Free Me From My Page

Aubrianna Rose

Copyright © 2018 by Aubrianna Rose

All rights reserved. No part of this book may be used or reproduced by any means, graphic, electronic, or mechanical, including photocopying, recording, taping or by any information storage retrieval system without the written permission of the author except in the case of brief quotations embodied in critical articles and reviews.

Because of the dynamic nature of the Internet, any web addresses or links contained in this book may have changed since publication and may no longer be valid. The views expressed in this work are solely those of the author.
The Author of this book does not dispense medical advice or prescribe the use of any technique as a form of treatment for physical, emotional, or medical problems without the advice of a physician, either directly or indirectly. The intent of the author is only to offer information of a general nature to help you in your quest for emotional and spiritual well-being. In the event you use any of the information in this book for yourself, which is your constitutional right, the author assumes no responsibility for your actions.

Printed in the United States of America.
Create Space rev. date: 2018

Cover art by Cover-Fish and Donya Sperry
Illustrations by Troy Jones

Dedication

I dedicate all my books to my kind and loving brother Mark Donavan Sperry who tragically left our planet far too early. Mark, my brother and close friend, you will endlessly be in my heart memory. I will Love you forever.

To everyone searching for Freedom and Liberty. Everyone desiring Empowerment. Everyone eager for Positive Change. Everyone, craving the understanding of Self-Love. To those desiring Vibrant Health and Authentic Happiness. Those tired of the stagnant boredom in their lives and ready for Change! And lastly, to those silently weeping, from behind the bars of their prison cages.

Contents

Chapter One: A Cold Winter Evening..................................1
Welcome to Lagunitas..6
Chapter Two: Early Memories.......................................7
Welcome to Sebastopol..24
Chapter Three: Memories on The Farm......................25
Chapter Four: Adventures in Every Corner...............38
Chapter Five: The Last of my Father's Rages!..........62
Welcome to Healdsburg...69
Chapter Six: Healdsburg..70
Chapter Seven: Me, Pretty?......................................86
Chapter Eight: My Wedding Day.............................101
Chapter Nine: My Cage..108
Chapter Ten: Our New Home...................................121
Chapter Eleven: Employment..................................144
Chapter Twelve: God Hates a Divorcing.................164
Chapter Thirteen: First Signs of Breakdown..........180
Chapter Fourteen: We Moved Again.......................185
Chapter Fifteen: Divorce..187
Chapter Sixteen: I Can't Believe My Eyes..............198
Chapter Seventeen: Breakdown..............................214
About the Author...233

Acknowledgments

My two amazing and patient young men — tired of hearing the same broken record: "Just a minute, I'm working on my book." Maximillian, my modern-day Mozart, artist, future book writer, counselor, and comedian. Tyler, my kind and caring athletic son. Possibly a future fire fighter or police officer. Tyler, like his older brother, also has the gift of humor. Our home has been known for lots and lots of laughter and I wouldn't want it any other way.

To my dear friend Anusha Amen Ra, who must have told me 10,000 times, "Breathe into your stomach, Aubri."

For Harris' consistent encouragement. "Write your book! Write your book! Write your book! Bri, are you working on your book?"

To my editors: Donya Sperry, Bill Chapman.

Foreword

Does time heal all wounds? The answer for each person is uniquely different. Some wounded individuals are not ready to pick up the shards of their broken life. So many pieces they're unsure, as they lay painfully in the middle of their shattered lives, just where to begin.

Sadly, for some individuals, overwhelming fear creates a barrier far too deep to penetrate. Their distress overrides any positivity, therefore disempowering them. Which in turn keeps a person emotionally frozen and in a cold world of their personal making. Which essentially is, non-growth.

Some yearn from a state of emotional isolation. They choose to no longer suffocate in stagnant chaos. Therefore, initiating their personal transformation and leaving behind a chaotic world. We find ourselves in the early stages of searching for freedom, and in doing so, we initiate our journey, our ascent out of darkness and into the light.

And now, I share with you my journey…

My Awakening

A sultry Summer evening in nineteen ninety-six. Tourists traveled from distant lands, both far and near, to view the splendors of Napa Valley.

Spring time. Mustard festivals, with miles upon endless miles of mustard growing tall and willowy, between vineyards and along country roadsides. A Yellow so exuberant in color, it would seem capable of lifting the last traces of winter's melancholy, in one thin inhale. Summer time. Brightly colored hot air balloons float high in the sky, while huffing and puffing a joyful rhythm. Fall time. Inhaling cool crisp air and marveling the rustic autumn colors, sprawling gracefully over valleys and hillsides. Regardless of the season, tourists explore wineries of undeniable distinction. Raising their wine glasses, while pondering the color, the scent, and savoring the taste.

In the meantime, while life's activities joyfully unfolded around me, my mind and body had been preparing for a terrifying and inescapable melt-down!

My life had slipped completely away from me, as though sand poured rapidly through the holes of a colander. I felt painfully empty and no longer able to hold my life together. At that very moment in time, every nerve and cell of my body crackled and popped as if water was thrown onto an electrical outlet.

Ten o'clock in the evening. Six months pregnant with my second child, alone in my home, and void of any light, except for that of the moon. Gasping and sobbing between cries, while trembling violently. Breathing was nearly impossible; as my chest tightened fiercely. On trembling legs, I climbed the stairs, entered the master bathroom, and stood before the mirror. A feeling of hysteria heightened to a sharp, and edgy peak, as I stared wildly into the eyes of a stranger. She dug her nails into her scalp and pulled at her waist length blonde hair. She then hurled out a terrifying scream:

"Please wont someone love me? I only want to be loved. Oh my God, oh my God, **oh...my...Goddd!!!**

Unable to stand any longer, she fell to her knees and onto the cool linoleum floor. Her heavy heart ached beyond words as she cried out again, "Won't someone please love me? Please, won't someone love me? I only want to be loved!"

She continued sobbing from her aching heart, with her face pressed against the floor in a puddle of tears. Gradually, her cries for love receded into shivering sobs and her convulsing gasps for air ceased.

Astonished, she felt an unusual sensation, so different from the emotions that had been ripping her apart earlier... she was no longer a terrified and lonely girl, in a pregnant woman's body. A calm and soothing warmth gently enveloped her, while a silent message repeated in her head:

"You're going to be alright, there's no need to worry... There's no need to worry."

It was as though the words radiated a warmth that penetrated straight to my bones.

And so, it was, on that Indian Summer evening, a slow and courageous journey began in her life. A seed so long parched, absorbed her desperate pleas for love and understanding, and pushed through the cracked sun baked earth, a tiny stem, holding tightly to an unfurled leaf.

How could a young woman, appearing to have it all, end up in this chaotic state? Explaining this in depth, requires peeling back the layers of her life, one tragedy at a time.

Chapter One
A Cold Winter Evening

My mother stood before the window, while contemplating the bone chilling December evening. The eerie wind swirled and whistled around our home like a groaning ghost, pulling and tugging at loose shingles and rattling mom's nerves.

"I never did like that sound. It frightens me; I wonder, will it rain? Do I need my umbrella?"

In the driveway, she saw the tail lights of the idling Oldsmobile station wagon. My Dad and family were waiting in the car. Dad never wanted us to be late. His impatience always had my family on edge. "This is the story of my life," he growled. "I'm always waiting on your mother."

Meanwhile, Mom was reluctant to leave our warm cozy house. *The cold air isn't good for the baby,* she thought. Nor was she looking forward to a two-hour Bible study with an hour of traveling over the icy mountain. She entertained the thought of staying in for the evening. Dreamily, she envisioned sitting by the warm glowing fire, sipping on her favorite gin and tonic cocktail with a slice of lime, "ahhh," she paused for one brief moment. When suddenly an obnoxious car horn jolted her back into cold reality.

"Come on, Marilyn! We'll be late!" he yelled. The horn blared a second time as he leaned into it for emphasis. Knowing full well he would leave if he had to wait too long, her heart raced. "He'll be so angry. Now, where did I put that diaper bag?" Nervously, she searched the room and caught sight of the pale green plastic bag under the baby's blanket on the sofa. Grabbing it, she nearly tripped in her black heels. With trembling hands, she checked the contents making sure she'd packed extra cloth diapers and a bottle of milk.

Hearing a chuckle, she turned around to see her amused father. He sat in his favorite old lounger, holding his ten-month-old, granddaughter on his lap. His two small grey poodles were sprawled on the floor, keeping warm by the fire as it crackled and popped. She looked at Aubrey's large blue eyes and amber colored locks, gazing up at her grandpa with adoration.

"What's so funny, Dad?"

Not taking his eyes off baby Aubri, he said, "Look at your mama. She's such a busy little thing. Why, she's as nervous as a cat thrown in a lake!" Aubri clutched her grandpa's lips while he spoke awkwardly through her curious fingers, "Are you going to be like that when you grow up?" "Gam-pa," she giggled.

"Oh, Dad," mother said, while rushing across the room to her teasing father. She scooped up the baby, bundled her in an oversized blanket, and hurried down the hall towards the front door. "See you in about three hours, dad."

"Okay darlin', enjoy your Bible class. It's a god awful cold night to be studying the Bible!" He exclaimed.

Reaching down, she clasped onto the cool metal knob and stepped outside into the cold. She held her baby tightly and ran awkwardly towards the car as the fierce arctic wind tugged at the baby's pink blanket. Her husband fixed his attention upon his wife. His anger faded as her beauty once again entranced him. Her shoulder length blonde hair blew wildly. Her black wool Chanel suit clung to the curves of her slender body.

"Phew," she exhaled, closing the door quickly.

"Well Blondie, I'm glad to see you made it," my grinning dad teased her.

"Ed, it's so cold. I was watching the news; they said it might reach freezing levels tonight! I sure hope the house will be warm when we get home!"

"Not to worry, Marilyn. I put an extra couple logs on before leaving," my dad assured her.

Mom, still clutching me close, turned around to inspect Ben, Susan and Liz. "Did you bring your Bible and song books?" she asked.

Inside the Kingdom Hall, Bible study was nearly ready to begin. Dad found a row of chairs and signaled mom to seat the children. From the congregation, girls stole shy glances of my dad—a handsome, rugged man, graced with a naturally muscular build, thick wavy auburn hair, and turquoise blue eyes. Women were always commenting, "Oh, my goodness, your dad looks just like Kirk Douglas."

The congregation had an interesting range of personalities. The arrogant ones with noses held high; the disgruntled ones, desiring to be anywhere else; the fearful, anxious ones; and the normal sort, appearing to have it all together—that would be me and my family.

Two hours passed; it was nearly 9:30. Although the room was filled with about seventy-five people, it remained relatively calm. Jehovah's Witnesses were instructed to keep their children silent. "Be quiet, sit still, or else." Or else what? Restless, frustrated children were taken out back and beat. There was no provision for a Sunday School for educating children about God in a fun way. From my experience, and I suspect I speak for thousands and thousands of children, this discipline had long-term damaging effects. I sat on my mother's lap chewing on a wooden spoon which also doubled as a disciplinary tool for my brother, sisters, and me. When suddenly, at the back of the room, the double doors were thrust open with a bang! The shocked congregation turned to see the cold blustery wind blow in a tall, stout policeman. His face was grim. The unexpected visitor bellowed out, "Is there an Edmond O'Brian here?" Mom tightened her grip around me as she stared in disbelief at my father. Equally shocked, Dad rose from his seat and walked to the back of the room. Hushed whispers filled the congregation as inquiring children tugged at their mothers' sleeves.

Dad approached the officer. "I'm Ed O'Brian," he replied.

The officer lowered his voice, but his brusque tone was audible. "Sorry to be the one to notify you Mr. O'Brian. Your house is on fire... It's too far gone for the crew to save!"

The congregation exploded in shocked gasps. Stares shifted to my stunned mom. "It must be a mistake!" she sputtered. "It can't be, it just can't be!" Then she gasped, "My Father!"

Later that evening, the wheels crunched into the gravel driveway. My Dad slowly brought the station wagon to a halt. My brother and sister's faces were pressed against the car window. Confusion and fear were my first recollections, as my Mother clutched me tightly, I heard her muffled cries from above as her chest heaved. Dad watched the devastation of our home, the home he had built, engulfed in ravenous flames lighting the night sky.

Painful expressions of defeat creased the faces of the fire crew. According to the inspection the following day, a strong gust of wind blew down the chimney creating sparks, some of which managed to enter the metal screen. Luckily, Grandpa stepped out to visit some friends. However, his two poodles did not survive.

The familiar comforts of our home were merely recollections. We stayed in neighbors' spare rooms that night. The following morning, my family was placed before "The Auctioneer." Who would take such a large family? We were sliced, diced and sold separately. My family stayed in donated rooms, motels, basements, and even a trailer for nearly a year. My Dad and brother Ben were separated from Mom and the girls.

It was sometime during the one-year separation from my Dad and brother Ben, that I was being sexually molested from a man. The beginning of my personal trauma memories were stored deeply in my sub-conscience, my "basement".

As devastating as these tragedies were, there was a much greater tragedy to befall my family— for underneath the appearance of the "perfect family" lay shame, humiliation, terrifying fear and guilt. All were products of my Dad's unpredictable rage and his faith in a religion that created debilitating fear and impossible demands upon their followers. And, my Mom's lack of love and understanding for her children's needs., as well as a nervous system, ready to implode at any moment.

Welcome To Lagunitas

Chapter Two

Early Memories

My family and I lived in a woodsy quiet mountain town of Lagunitas, California. The town consisted of: one general store, with post office combined. When I was three years old, we moved a second time, into our new home which my father also built, on the corner of Arroyo Drive. Down the road from us, lived a famous rock group of the sixties and seventies, *The Grateful Dead*, my big brother Ben thought it was "totally groovy."

Lagunitas had what all children dreamed of: a river. During the cold rainy months of Winter, the lazy babbling river became a raging torrent! Throughout the warm, sultry summer months, water poured calmly over moss covered rocks. Sprightly skipper bugs danced across the water, while tadpoles darted in and out of muddy hideaways and narrowly escaping children's squealing attempts at catching them. Let's never forget, one of my favorites: the rhythmic call of crickets and delightful sound of croaking bull frogs.

Some neighbors found our home so large, they named it "the battleship." What dad designed and built was a stylish French blue ranch house with white trim. A spacious front porch was made of aged red brick. Inside, we had an open living room with a bay window and a built-in bench seat overlooking our front yard.

My parents' room, the master suite, was elegant with a 1930's Art Deco bedroom set. The scalloped head board, covered in rose colored crushed velvet, stood an impressive five feet high. The comforter and pillows complemented in golden mauve silk with a matching queen's royalty chair. Like each bedroom, the master bedroom came complete with an intercom to keep close tabs on everyone. The master bathroom was a statement of Dad's desire to indulge my Mom. Blue tiles stepped down into a Roman sunken tub where water poured out of golden faucets; it took nearly an hour to fill. Although the entire family could have fit in it together, it was exclusively for Mom and Dad.

A white picket fence enclosed the front yard's sprawling green lawn. A creek flowed through our back yard and under a small rustic bridge. Over time, the creek became my enchanting secret hideaway.

There I am. Do you see me, over there, by the water's edge? I'm the barefoot child wearing red shorts and a dirtied yellow t-shirt. I'm holding a pale green 7-Up bottle and stuffing a scrawled message into the neck of it. The paper reads, *Hi, I'm Aubri, call me when you find this note*. While biting the corner of my lip, I push the cork into the neck and place my sacred glass bottle into the swift moving water. I hold my breath as it drifts downstream, swirling around white frothy bubbles and narrowly escaping threatening boulders and logs. I imagine the bottle making its way into the hands of another child on the other side of the world, as all children innocently believe!

If I wasn't playing in the creek, I was sure to be swimming in our pool. At the bottom of our pool, four large tiled fish flickered and shimmered iridescent shades of emerald green and aqua blue. I delighted in tossing a penny into the water. As my copper treasure made its way to the bottom, I'd plug my nose and jump in feet first. Down into a silent, fluid world I plunged, as millions of gurgling bubbles raced past me to the water's surface.

Danger Will Robinson!

Even at the early age of three, I had an innate instinct to protect. Whether it was wounded birds, wounded dogs, or wounded people, I felt I simply must help, it was a nature, which ran deeply with in my core.

One summer afternoon, while in the kitchen sipping cherry Kool Aid from a paper cup, I fantasized over my favorite scary show: *Lost in Space.* The Robinson family could never seem to find their way home. I thought of Will and his friend the robot, everyone should have a defending robot-like Will's, *"danger, Will Robinson, Danger!"* My day dreaming of another planet, ended when I heard strange laughter from outside. I hurried to the window to investigate. Dad and a friend were in the back yard boxing. It didn't look like they were being nice to each other. I watched in horror as the man lunged and swung his fist into Dad's head. A wave of panic and heat washed over me. I dropped my paper cup onto the white linoleum floor, red Kool Aid splashed, as my bare feet slid in the sweet mess towards the back door. While shuving the screen door open in a frenzy, I thought of one thing only: Saving my Daddy! The screen slammed shut behind me with a bang!

Blood trickled out of my Dad's nose and all down his face. In horror, I ran straight at the man, and screamed with all my might "Leave my Daddy alone! Leave him alone! Tears rolled down my cheeks as I begged and pleaded to the man hurting my Daddy to stop. Mom immediately put the "boy's" games to rest.

Potty Trained?

One afternoon when I was three years old, I joyfully rooted through the white toy chest in our bedroom, in search of the little wooden car with faded red paint and yellow wheels. I tossed behind me Mr. Potato Head, Legos, Barbies, and others onto the blue-gray carpet. While I continued rummaging, the flash of a yellow wheel under a Raggedy Ann doll caught my attention. Satisfied, I sat down on the plush rug and played with the car. I had not been playing for long when I heard my Dad hollering from the other end of the house. As his yelling got louder, my nerves shook, and my stomach tightened. He entered my room, his face red with anger as he yelled out my name. Frightened and confused, I jumped up on trembling legs and looked up at him. My fear caused me to lose control of my bladder. Urine ran down my legs and puddled beneath my bare feet. When he saw what I had done, his anger escalated. Next thing I remember, he was down on his knees aggressively shoving my face back and forth into the urine-soaked carpet, forcing the warm fluid into my mouth and nostrils. "What do ya think you are," he yelled with seething anger, "a dog or cat that needs to be potty trained?"

I still haven't a clue what a three-year-old could have done to set off such rage. Eventually, I learned not to express my feelings; they should never be independent of my Dad's! So, what did I do? I shoved my emotions and frustrations deep into the pit my stomach.

Even today as I recall that memory, I wonder, was it because of Mom's, constant threats "just wait till your father gets home!" We'd done nothing out of the normal for two or three-year-old children. One afternoon Susan and I asked if we could share a piece of French bread. she said yes, but when we had two pieces, the threat of our Dad coming home and beating us with a belt was hanging over our heads. So, possibly that was the day I had to much French bread with Susan.

Bible Study

One day a week, we studied the Bible in my Dad's office above his garage. He expected my siblings and I to pay attention and have an answer ready, or we'd be spanked. I wasn't in school yet, therefore I didn't know how to read, however I knew he meant what he said. Because I was terrified of his discipline, I memorized what I was hearing while Ben or Susan read. While sitting on the floor of his office and trying to remember every word, I developed an odd habit. I swallowed tiny silver nuts and bolts which I found on the floor. The cool sensation of them slowly sliding down my throat somehow comforted me. When it was time for bed, I developed another unusual habit: I found pleasure in sinking my teeth into the solid maple bed frame. Feeling and hearing the crunching sound was oddly comforting. In time, the headboard was covered in teeth impressions. I worried that Mom would find them, but surprisingly, she never did. These memories I share, are early signs, of a severely frustrated child.

My First Sleep Over

At times, I seriously needed an escape from Dad's unpredictable anger. Anytime I had the opportunity to spend the night at a friend's house, I would take it. I will always remember my first sleepover and dinner at my best friend Jennifer's home. Her mother Evelyn amazed me. She was around fifty years old but looked to be seventy. She held in one hand a cigarette and in the other a tall glass filled with whiskey and soda water. We sat at the dinner table eating fried chicken with mashed potatoes and brown gravy. Suddenly, Jennifer's mother deliberately spit out her dentures — both upper and lower. On to the table they dropped! Seeing my horrified expression, she threw back her head and cackled a toothless roar of laughter. That was my first introduction to false teeth. Not pleasant, not, not, not!

Years later, when I'd see commercials advertising denture cream and seeing an elderly person chomping his or her pearly whites into a corn cob dripping with butter, I think of Evelyn. It was not just fried chicken served for dinner that night; it was dinner and a show!

Free Me From My Cage

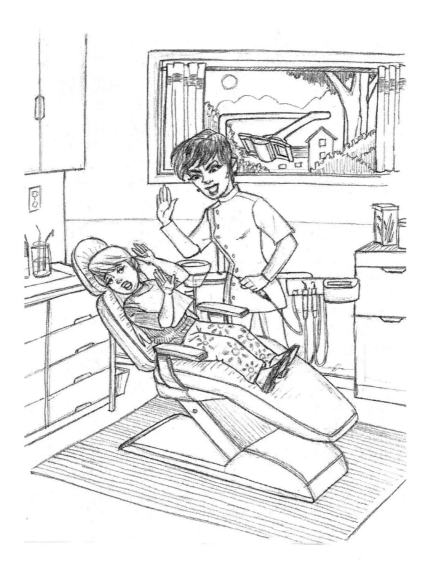

Shut Up!

Although, this memory is also about teeth, it was shocking and hardly humorous. I was five years old and complained of a toothache, so my Mom took me to my first dentist appointment. We sat on cold metal chairs in a large brightly lit room.

I heard my name announced by a tall, wiry woman at the far end of the corridor. Her tone of voice and facial expression frightened me. I looked at my Mom; she instructed me to go to the woman. Hesitantly, I walked down the long hall. The woman walked impatiently in front of me. I scrambled to keep up with her on the slippery floor. I followed her into a room and was overwhelmed by a strong smell of medicine. Pointing at a large chair, she ordered me to sit in it. She looked irritated while yanking my long hair out of her way and clipping a paper bib onto my collar. Next, she slammed frightening tools onto a metal tray in front of me.

With absolutely no forewarning, she grabbed my mouth and told me to open wide. She forced a foreign object into my mouth, which caused me to gag. She then slapped me hard across my face and told me to stop gagging. I was terrified of this cruel woman and fought back the tears pricking at my eyes and the natural urge to gag. I held my breath and squeezed my eyes tightly shut. But the gag came anyway. She slapped again, and harder. Horrified, I cried out for my mother. She clasped her hand tightly over my mouth and growled a bitter voice in my ear: "You better shut up now, do you hear me?"

She released her hand instantly and forced a plastic smile when a man dressed in white entered the room. That horrible woman kept me from ever complaining of toothaches again.

First Day of School

My first day of school. Our bus stopped just outside the front door at our white picket fence. While I waited with curious excitement beside Liz, my more experienced sister, for she had ridden the bus before. Anxiously and with great anticipation, I wondered when our bus would come. Then, there she came, in all her yellow glory. I practically jumped out of my favorite black patent leather shoes. The bright happy bus pulled up to our gravel driveway, and a cloud of dust formed as squeaky brakes brought her to a halt. The powerful doors thrust open and up the stairs went Liz with me right on her heels. The bus was filled with noisy children. Liz found a seat next to a blonde-haired boy, leaving me alone. Frightened, I walked towards the back of the bus. Sitting by herself was a pretty black girl about my age. I was startled by her color and reluctant to sit next to her, because she was the first black person I had ever seen. Had it been today, I would have smiled and said, "Hi, I'm Aubri, can I sit with you?" But sadly, I kept walking.

We arrived at the San Geronimo Elementary School. Feeling scared and uncertain, I finally found the office. The secretary instructed me to sit down and then proceeded to barrage me with questions: what shots I had, what was my address, phone number, and emergency contacts. My reply for each question stayed consistent: "Hmm, I don't know." It turned out, my Mom had never enrolled me.

Free Me From My Cage

Easter Performance

In the spring, my teacher organized an Easter pageant; I was excited beyond words! The evening performance had finally arrived. We had practiced faithfully for weeks before our debut. My entire first grade class was singing on the stage, I stood right in the middle. I was wearing my favorite yellow dress with a scalloped lace collar, black patent leather shoes, and white anklet socks. My face beamed with joy, I wanted to burst into giggles. I felt as though I could take off and fly! We sang of pink tulips, yellow daffodils, fluffy hopping bunnies, and butterflies.

While singing, I scanned the audience looking for my family. *They'll be so proud of me*, I thought. And there in the crowd of faces was Dad, angry and scowling. *What did I do wrong now?* Everything around me blurred; even the voices of the children sounded far away. I felt a tightness in my tummy; the singing no longer mattered. After the red curtain dropped, the next thing I remember we were in the station wagon headed home.

Dad spoke angrily to my Mom, while my brother and sisters nervously listened. "Marilyn, what the hell were you thinking? We don't celebrate Easter. Why did you let Aubri sing in the play?" Mom explained she didn't know it was an Easter performance. "Well, maybe you should pay more attention next time," he growled. Sadly, I took on the shame and guilt for something I didn't understand. We were not allowed to perform in school functions that had anything to do with holidays. We never celebrated birthdays, Thanksgiving, Christmas, Halloween, etc.... My punishment for singing in the Easter play was, no dessert when we got home.

Thirty-Eight Years Later

Thirty-eight years later, I overcame another childhood trauma. I joined a Renaissance Christmas pageant. The performance was held in a historic Methodist church complete with an authentic bell tower that tolls before Sunday's service. The halls were decorated in 13th century motif — the age of kings, queens and brave-hearted knights. My fellow comrades were well trained in the fields of acting and singing. As for me, I didn't know how to read music and had never taken acting or singing lessons before. However, my biggest challenge was, learning the Christmas songs. I had to keep reminding the cast, "Hey guys, don't forget I used to be a Jehovah's Witness." My legitimate excuse for fumbling through the words.

My inner nagging voice used this as the perfect opportunity to creep into my psyche with a down-load of negative influence. *You're not good enough, give up, you have no talent, you don't know how to sing, and besides that, it's Pagan*! The word Pagan rang loudly in my head! I have learned from experience, when this nagging intruder raises its destructive voice, I must turn the volume off! and replace it with my higher voice—the voice of wisdom, the voice of encouragement! The voice of Love!

As a newbie, I received the role of what we call the Head Mistress, in which I was required to learn the longest opening lines, as well as several other bits throughout the performance. On opening night, I was so nervous that I mixed a spoonful of rum in my mug of warm apple cider and I repeated it the following four evening shows. Some of the cast members would stroll towards me with raised mug in hand and a twinkle in their eyes. "Ahhh," I'd say with a wink, then discreetly top their mugs off with a splash! One evening before opening performance, I told Bob, one of our cast members, "I can do this on my own! I know I can! I'm not spiking my cider tonight!"

"Hey, there you go. I know you can do it, too!" He smiled.

Before stepping on stage, I silently repeated to myself with conviction over and over again, *"I can do this, I can do this, I know I can".*

And... I did, just like I knew I could!

We sang, danced, and acted, the applause was unbelievably rewarding! I was given hugs and told how graceful and talented I am; some even asked me how long I had lived in the States. Apparently, my Scottish brogue was quite convincing. Joining the Christmas singing, and acting group was truly one of the best things I could have done for my five-year old girl. And... I even got to have, dessert!

Arroyo Drive

Mom brought her fifth child into the world—the most beautiful, round faced, blonde angel, I had ever seen: Luke Donavan. I remember the day Mom brought him home from the hospital. Swaddled in a cozy blue blanket, he had one eye open and the other tightly shut. Concerned, I asked Mom, "What's wrong with his other eye?"

My last memory in this home on Arroyo Drive was disappointing, and one most families go through at some point. I remember the day well. Swinging on the swing set, in our back yard, I swayed back and forth singing the theme song *Hey, Hey We're the Monkeys* from the new TV show, *Oh, how dreamy Davey Jones is.* I visualized the two of us together, my lips near his. He leans in closer to me and whispers in my ear... "Aubrianna, come in the house, your father wants to have a talk with everyone." Regrettably, I walked to the house leaving dreamy Davey and the kiss behind.

Dad gathered all of us together at the dining room table. He had never done this before unless we were having a Bible study, which had us all sitting up straight and paying attention. His tone was serious, and his face creased with burden and disappointment. He told us his construction work had slowed down. "We'll be moving to a second home of ours in Sebastopol about an hour north. I think you'll like it. It's in the country with lots of land."

So, my family and I moved again. Little did I know, my years on the farm would bring such joy and pain.

Welcome to Sebastopol

Chapter Three
Memories on The Farm

Ahhh... Sebastopol. Its focus: apples! Once a year in April, Sebastopol honors the apple blossom with an extravagant festival, starting with an exciting parade marching down the main street. Countless booths are scattered about. Local artists' paintings, photography, pottery, and more. There are limitless choices of mouthwatering goodies, apple cobblers, apple turnovers, apple butter, apple jam, candied apples, and apple pies. You name it, and apples are a part of it.

So, it probably won't surprise you to learn that our new home in the country was surrounded by six acres of apple trees! Across the street from us was an apple juice factory. Our long gradually sloping gravel driveway had hundreds of golden delicious trees on the left of us, and on the right, a row of majestic Monterey Cypress trees, which separated our property line, from the abandoned school house and our neighbor, Mr. Bubbles (I'll introduce you to him later).

We had six acres of apple trees, eight walnut trees, two orange trees, three lemon trees, a cherry tree in need of serious pruning, and two palm trees standing over one hundred feet tall, and one of them housing a family of owls. I was thrilled to discover another creek at the bottom of the hill just past the Gravenstein apple trees. The creek had tall stately Redwood trees that lined both sides of the bank.

Our home, a rustic, yet charming 1940's farm house: white with green trim, with a full-length

front porch — the kind straight out of an old-time movie, as you relax in a rocking chair sipping from your chilled glass of Mint Julep tea. The porch overlooked our sprawling green lawn with a tulip tree filled with purple blossoms in the spring.

Inside, our family room had maple hardwood flooring. The only source for heating our home was an enormous floor heater in one corner of the room. On chilly mornings, my sisters, Luke, and I stood with trembling legs over the metal grate while we got dressed for school. Some of us, would spit so we could hear the sizzle of saliva hitting the hot metal.

As I mentioned, our home was rustic; however, the charming part didn't come till later. Liz, Susan, and I shared our cold and drafty room which had a one-inch crack in the wall; we could actually see outside. Dad covered the crack with plastic until he was able to repair it. My parent's room, shared with my baby brother Luke, had no door; their only privacy was a shower curtain. And, our entire family shared one tiny bathroom.

The kitchen was a bright and sunny room with large picture windows, which had outdoor planter boxes overflowing with Mom's summer favorites: white daisies, pink and red petunias, and blue salvia. Our oven was considered an antique even for the 1960's: a chipped, white porcelain stove standing on four legs. It had two options for cooking: firewood or gas flame. It came complete with a built-in skillet for frying our favorites — sausage and Johnny cakes — unless Mom used wood for heating, then they weren't much to be desired, they were either burned on the outside or raw and gooey on the inside.

Off the kitchen was our walk-in pantry, and ironing room. Through the years, my sisters and I spent many hours pressing, starching, and steaming wrinkled clothing, into wrinkle free submission.

We had a basement below the kitchen, and the only access to the basement, was from outside. It was dimly lit and smelled oddly of dust, laundry detergent, damp earth, and oak barrels filled with Dads famous red wine. Mom had ample space for shelving her mason jars filled with summer vegies. The basement also had a shower, sink, and toilet, all in the open with no walls for privacy.

Roughly fifty yards away from the farm house stood our aged, yet stately two-story tank house. Both levels had been converted into bedrooms. My older brother Ben was lucky enough to get the best bedroom of all: the top story! My sisters and I enjoyed sleeping in the lower level during the warm summer months. We could goof off and giggle and not worry about getting into trouble (except for that one night, I'll share with you later). Neither room came equipped with a bathroom, and the farmhouse basement was too far away, "for a gotta tinkle now!" So, we were known to use the sand box my father built for Luke, just a stone's throw away.

Down the hill was our large and rustic red barn. The only things missing in Dad's "living on the farm" vision, were animals, which were soon to come!

Dad and Grandma

My Grandma Elizabeth, lived in Oakland, California. Because she was a busy woman, we didn't get to see her much. A tall slender woman with long wavy brown hair, which she mostly wore in a "Gibson Girl" bun, her face was beautiful, and she had a most captivating smile.

Dad and Grandma did not get along well; they had a difference of opinion, especially where religion was concerned. Grandma was a devoted Christian Science healing practitioner. So, when my Dad left his Christian Science faith, to join a religion of his choice, Grandma wasn't happy!

My Dad said he didn't know about the Great Depression going on in the world because they always had food on the table and a maid to care for him while his ma was at work. Grandma was a secretary. At one time, they lived in Oregon, where she became the state secretary for the Governor of Oregon. She also owned a lumber and mill yard. Money never seemed to be an issue.

She divorced my Grandfather in the 1930's which was unheard of then. After many years of being single, she eventually remarried in her 50's. He was older than Grandma by fifteen or more years, he was a retired politician. Oh, how I loved my Grandpa Perry, a kind and gentle man. I loved sitting in his lap when he smoked his pipe, which smelled deliciously of cinnamon, licorice, and woodsy oak. Grandma was most noted to her grandchildren for making our favorite: homemade vanilla ice cream and her famous lemon meringue pie.

Because Dad and Grandma had a difference of opinion regarding religion, it usually meant there was an underlying tension between two strong willed, Scotch Irish temperaments with a fighting passion for their God, which caused them to be anything but "Christ-like." Visualize two male rams charging each other full speed, and that would-be Grandma and Dad. I remember one day she was supposed to spend a weekend with us; however, she left the same day she came, she didn't approve of our religion and refused to reason with my Dad.

Kitchen Memories

Our kitchen, the heart of our home. Winter months were especially warm and cozy. On Mondays, Mom would make homemade bread.

After school, I stepped quickly off the bus in my over-sized green rubber boots. Through puddles I splashed! And, in muddy orchards I slipped! While awkwardly running in my older sister's Liz's hand me down boots. I had one goal in mind: warm delicious bread smothered in butter. When finally, in the house, I'd rip off my boots and charge across the hardwood floor. The delicious aroma of baking bread was overwhelming as several loaves of bread cooled.

Our kitchen was an enjoyable place to be during the warm summer months as well. Mom did an enormous amount of canning from the garden's endless supply of carrots, zucchini, tomatoes, corn bell peppers, and much more. You name it and she was canning it.

One memorable late evening I will always hold dear to my heart, mainly because my mother ordinarily would not let me do this. She was now pregnant with her sixth child—my soon to be baby sister Anne. It was the only time she allowed me to help her in the kitchen so late at night. The entire family was asleep. Quietly, we worked alongside each other as we rinsed, sliced, de-stemmed, and peeled veggies.

Even the clean-up was fun. I heaped all the veggie scraps into my red egg collecting basket and walked down the sloping hill to the hen yard. The sultry still night air smelled of hay and apples while nature slept in a muted moonlit haze of tranquility. I felt on this one evening that all was right in the world. A curious feeling of calm settled comfortably within, as I quietly scattered the chicken's vegie scraps.

Although Mom was a good cook, when her grocery budget was slim, she made her usual: beans! Don't even think of whining, "ohhh no, beans again ma?" It meant for an extremely sore butt and straight to bed we'd go. (Maybe that wasn't such a bad idea.)

So, on bean night, whomever set the dinner table knew the rules: place extra napkins at each table setting (except Mom and Dads of course.) The napkins were used for discreetly spitting our beans into. Those of us nervous of being caught with loaded napkins (that would be me) chose another technique.

I had managed to refine the art of bean swallowing, before my gag reflex kicked in. With a tall glass filled with water in one hand and a spoon heaped with those god-awful lentils in the other, I nervously glanced over my shoulder to see if Mom or Dad were watching! I plugged my nose and shoveled those slimy beans down. As I recall these memories, it surprises me that my parents were unaware of the disappearing bean act or the kitchen trash filled and weighted down with soggy, bean-filled napkins.

Another meal, or should I say banquet, has my family still talking about today. On the rare occasion my family stayed home from our usual Saturday morning door-to-door preaching, Mom prepared a breakfast feast: platters piled high with buckwheat pancakes and waffles, warmed syrup, bowls heaped with whipped cream and garden-fresh strawberries, sausage, eggs, country fried potatoes, and pitchers filled with fresh cow's milk and orange juice. Needless to say, lunch was not served on those days.

Mom Ahead of Her Time

Mom was ahead of her time; a true pioneer of health and nutrition. She taught my siblings and me the value of plants, herbs, and the healing benefits provided from nature's medicine. Being raised in the 1970's health food stores were not like they are today. I called them hippy stores, they all seemed to smell the same—of pungent body odor, incense and musky patchouli oil.

On visits to the local health food store, Mom had me scoop cayenne pepper and golden seal powder from bins and place them into plastic bags. When we got home, she had me pour the contents into separate small bowls and a third bowl for gelatin capsules. I filled each capsule with the herbs, a slow tedious chore which left my fingertips stained yellow and red. I learned how the medicine in cayenne pepper helps improve circulation and relieves headaches. Golden Seal is highly esteemed for its ability to heal skin disease, nausea, common colds and so forth.

Mom had several fascinating books on healing. Because that sort of reading material would have been considered Demonic, she kept them discreetly tucked away from the eyes of fellow Jehovah's Witnesses. Had mom lived in Salem a few hundred years ago, she would have been called a "witch" and burned at the stake. Even yoga was considered demonic. I was told by my Dad and elders in our congregation, "Because yoga calms your mind, the demons have easier access for entering."

As I presently reason with such an absurd comment, I ask. "How can a religion make such blatant, obtrusive, and inaccurate statements such as those?" Yoga is an exercise that stretches, tones, and strengthens our bodies. When taught to breathe properly and relax deeply, one can relieve anxiety and panic attacks, overcome trauma, lower blood pressure, balance the right and left-brain hemispheres and more. Technically speaking, with that sort of ridiculous reasoning, wouldn't we be more susceptible for Satanic influence when we're sleeping?

As a child, my Mom wasn't one to hold me, tell me she loved me, or show me any form of affection. So, you can imagine, how rare those memories with Mom were. I'll fondly embrace: canning in the kitchen that one late Summer evening; Mondays after school, smelling the heavenly aroma of home baked bread; her amazing Buffet Saturdays; my red and orange stained finger tips, reminding me of the healing benefits of herbs. Those times in the kitchen will be forever etched in the corner of my mind. Thank you, Mom, for those valuable skills you taught me.

Chores

My siblings and I never wanted to displease our parents. The discipline was frightful, not to mention unbearable. It was challenging to gauge my Dad's fiery anger. So, we always completed all chores, and there were always plenty of chores to do: weeding the lawn, weeding the vegetable garden, washing dishes, feeding the chickens, cleaning the chicken coop, collecting the eggs, washing the eggs, ironing, sweeping, stacking fire wood, and the endless list went on and on and on.

Some chores were fun, such as butter churning. Ben milked Bessie at six a.m. every morning before school. Once a week, we would make butter. Mom separated the cream from the milk by scooping the layer of foamy cream floating on top into a porcelain pitcher. After school, the pitcher of cream was waiting in the refrigerator. I poured the cream into a half gallon glass container, placed four wooden beaters attached to the lid into the glass jar, and screwed it shut. I went outside onto the back-porch and sat in the warm sunshine and began churning. Making butter took strength and determination! Turning the handle in a circular motion, the beaters began to spin. As the mixture thickened, the handle was more difficult to turn. Roughly a half hour later, I returned to the kitchen, removed the lid, and scraped the contents off the beaters and from inside the jar into a bowl.

And, presto! we had butter! I never cared for it though, because it tasted and smelled more like cheese.

Vegetable Garden

Midway down the hill, just past the red barn, was a large plot of freshly plowed earth with cow manure added for nitrates. Because my Dad was born in the city, an over-sized garden was important to him. Although he didn't have much knowledge of gardening, he was fully capable of learning from experienced friends, and in a short time he learned a great deal.

My favorite chore was planting vegetable seeds. Spreading soil over the top, patting it with gentle care. Then water, and wait, and wait, and wait a little more. For ten days or longer, depending on which seeds I had planted, I'd run down the hill to see my seedlings. One afternoon, I finally saw the young tender green sprouts poking their heads up out of the dirt. I squealed with laughter! "Ahhh... you're so cute!"

When mature, our plot of rich soil looked like a master garden with several rows of corn, potatoes, bell peppers, artichokes, peas, tomatoes, cucumbers, zucchini, carrots — the list of vegetables went on and on, as did the watering and weeding. Chores occupied an enormous amount of our time. When dad asked me to water the garden — that was an hour. And, when dad asked me to weed the rows of corn? Oh, my lord, that alone was a five-day chore!

After my chores were completed each day, I ran as fast as I could from Mom's hawk eye or Dad's, deep holler.

Regardless of my Dad's unpredictable rage and his attempts to break me in, as though I were a wild horse, nearly all my fondest childhood memories were spent there, on the farm. I found joy and enchantment nearly everywhere.

Aubrianna Rose

Ahhh... What magical place calls to me today? It seemed as if there were adventures in every corner of our six-acre farm that awaited my discovery!

Free Me From My Cage

Chapter Four
Adventures in Every Corner

One summer afternoon, I was busy completing one of my chores, which happened to be ironing. The heavy steel iron hissed, while swirling steam reddened my cheeks, the relaxing routine was interrupted, by a knock at the front door. Leaving the pile of clothing behind, I went to investigate who was at the door. It was Mr. Bubbles, our neighbor. He towered over me. I had never seen him up close before. I stood staring up at him, my mouth wide open. "Good afternoon," he smiled. His face was wrinkled like a prune, his few remaining teeth were discolored, and he reeked of body odor and cigarette smoke. He wore oversized trousers held up with suspenders and a dirty white t-shirt stretched tightly over his protruding pot belly. I didn't know whether to feel sorry or disgusted with him.

He lived in a trailer that leaned at a slight angle, which appeared in desperate need of repair! (Or, a bulldozing!) In his side yard, tied with a lead rope to his porch railing, was his spunky Shetland pony, named Shorty. He had come to ask my Dad's permission to board his pony in our corral. My Dad was pleased to help his neighbor and add another animal to the farm. So, adventures on the farm began.

Ben and my sisters were planning to ride Shorty, regardless of the fact that Shorty had not been ridden in years and we didn't have a saddle or reins. Ben bravely volunteered to climb on first; his long legs touched the ground. He barely had a chance to grab on when off that pony charged, kicking and bucking. Ben rolled off Shorty's back squealing with laugher. My two older sisters Liz and Susan were next in line; one by one, they met their fate.

Now it was my turn. The bleachers were crowded with people cheering me on. The rodeo clown stood poised and ready to distract the bull. Anxiously, I sat on the fence awaiting Ben's instructions, the pony cornered beneath me. I lowered myself onto the snorting, thrashing little beast, wrapped my legs tightly around his warm belly, and twisted the wiry hair of his mane around my fists.

Ben smiled, "Are you ready?"

Nervously I answered, "Yes."

Ben loosened his grip from around Shorty's neck and quickly moved out of his way, when off ran that short, stubborn little devil. My body was tossed about like a limp rag doll. Shorty headed straight for the gnarled, dried out walnut tree; the branches hung low like an old witch's hand. Wickedly, she cackled as she reached her crooked hands out and scraped me off. I hit the ground hard, the wind was knocked out of me. My face and arms were scratched, and pieces of leaves and tree branches were stuck in my hair. While spitting dirt out of my mouth, I wondered, *"What happened to the rodeo clown?"* So... The stubborn pony's mission was accomplished; no one ever attempted straddling Shorty again.

Henrietta

In time, many animals lived on our farm: pigs, rabbits, cows, chickens, dogs, cats, geese, ducks, and that stubborn pony named Shorty, (you know the one!) One of the ducks had become a proud mother for the first time. Her name was Henrietta and she guarded her ducklings well. I desired more than anything to hold and cuddle one of her adorable babies; they waddled around like little balls of yellow fluff. Henrietta strutted around the barn yard with beak held high, as though born of nobility. A short, white, plump English Countess, protecting her young. Anytime I was remotely close to her ducklings, Henrietta ran me off as though I were beneath her webbed feet. *Stay away, peasant girl*, she quacked.

So, it was time the peasant girl outsmarted the prideful one. It just so happened Henrietta's weakness was dog food. That's right, the noble girl liked dog food. She was notorious for chasing the dogs away from their food and scarfing down the dry morsels as fast as her beak allowed.

Down into the basement I ran, in search of the golden ticket. I grabbed two heaping handfuls from the large bag on the floor. Smugly, I walked up the basement stairs! Now, prepared with the eyes of a hawk and the poise of a panther, I went in search of Henrietta. *"There she is; my mission is nearly complete".* Cautiously, I approached her, took a deep breath, raised my hands slowly into the air and threw the food in front of her. She momentarily lost her senses as she waddled at top speed and joyously quacked in the direction of tasty morsels raining out of the sky. My hawk eyes zeroed in on the closest victim. I swooped down, grasped the duckling, and ran with the speed of a panther!

Henrietta halted her scarfing when she heard her baby's squeaks of protest. Her waddling was surprisingly fast, but not fast enough to outrun the panther. Sprinting back down the steps and into the basement, I quickly shut the door behind me!

Outside the door, Henrietta demanded her baby back with loud authoritative outbursts. The tiny guy shrieked at me the thief. My vision of cuddling the adorable yellow duckling quickly faded as I realized it was more fun to look at than to hold. I waited for Henrietta to calm down before returning her baby. She was grateful to have her duckling back and I was relieved to have all ten fingers.

Henrietta's motto was: *You can look, but don't touch my babies.*

More Happiness in Giving

One sunny afternoon, I sat crouched near a spring-fed brook, which slowly trickled down and around patches of wild watercress. Reaching down, I gently tugged a single stem from the cool water and dreamily placed it in my mouth, gradually chewing my way up the sweet tender reed. I reached down for another when a flash of turquoise beneath the water caught my attention. I pulled up a beautiful stone the size of a quarter. *It's perfect*, I thought. Thrilled and excited, I splashed barefoot through the cool water to the other side.

While clutching firmly my new-found treasure, I sprinted through the apple orchard, my toughened feet ran over the sun baked clumps of hardened dirt, left behind from the tractor rototilling. Excited, I crossed the lawn and charged up the front porch steps. I headed straight to my bedroom in search of a secret hiding place. *Umm ... where to hide it*, I wondered. Suddenly, I heard my brother Luke asking, "Whatcha doin?" I held out my hand with delight showing him what I'd found. His eyes brightened! And, in a quick instant, his chubby fingers latched onto it. "This rock is pretty," he giggled. "I want it."

"No, Luke," I replied, "I found it in the creek. It's very special to me." He stubbornly tightened his fist. "Please Luke let me have it back" I calmly tried reasoning with him. He wouldn't open his fist. So, I pried it loose from his surprisingly strong grip. I exhaled a relief, "phew", and held my turquoise gem again. What happened next, was what all typical three-year old's do: Luke became a raging little maniac! "I WANT YOUR SPECIAL ROCK, I WANNA HOLD IT," he bellowed!

I attempted to calm him; yet, he had no intention of stopping. As his tantrum escalated, I heard a roar much louder than my brother's as Dad entered the room. "What the hell is going on in here?" He roared!

Luke continued shrieking, "I WANT YOUR ROCK AUBRI".

Even though I was terrified of Dad's rage, I tried reasonably explaining the situation to him. His face reddened with anger as he interrupted my nervous attempts. He reached down and grabbed me by my shirt collar and lifted me off the floor inches away from his rage. He held me so close to his angry face I could see his tonsils and felt heat spewing from his twisted mouth. He bellowed out a scripture with unrelenting rage, "THE BIBLE SAYS THERE IS MORE HAPPINESS IN GIVING THEN IN RECEIVING. NOW, GIVE HIM THAT DAMN ROCK OR I'LL SHOVE IT DOWN YOUR THROAT! DO YOU HEAR ME?"

Horrified and barely able to reply, I managed a feeble, "Yes, I hear you." He set me down on trembling legs. In a state of shock and once again feeling severely wounded, I handed Luke my treasure. *How can a father quote a scripture with such rage? Jesus taught us, to love one another, not to have blind rage.*

Aubrianna Rose

Another Day in the Hen House

One of my chores, was hands down, one of the most challenging: Which was, collecting the eggs from the hen house. After gathering eggs, I'd walk up the hill to the farm house basement, then I'd wash and dry them, gently place them in egg cartons, so we could later sell them for fifty cents a dozen.

It's necessary to collect the eggs everyday otherwise they become fertile and a small speck of blood, the early stage of an embryo, forms inside the egg. The longer the hen sits on her eggs, the bigger the spot becomes. It's not a pleasant thing to see when you're making an omelet.

Mom had become accustomed to the amount of eggs I would bring home every day. If I missed any, she'd know from the spot inside the egg. She'd then question it over dinner in Dad's presence. Not wanting to displease my dad, my search for eggs became fear driven.

The following day, I heaved the enormous heavy barn door open as it creaked and swayed slowly. The light inside the barn was dim except for the occasional beams of sunlight streaming down from cracks in the ceiling. An unusual mixture of odors was oddly comforting to me: tractor oil, alfalfa hay and manure. The barn had a life of its own—cows, chickens, birds chirping in the rafters above, and a plump cat crouched near a hole poised and ready to pounce on an unsuspecting mouse.

Nonchalantly, I entered the chicken coop at the far end of the barn. Cautiously, I watched my step, trying to avoid slipping in wet chicken poop. Approaching the empty nests, I gathered the brown eggs, placing them gently in my basket. I became aware of an odd sensation as though something was tickling me.

Dismissing it, I continued gathering eggs when I felt this strange sensation a second time. Looking into my basket at the eggs, I noticed in disgust they were covered in tiny, white, nearly microscopic bugs. Millions of bugs were crawling everywhere. I watched in horror at the chickens trying to shake off the creepy crawlies.

The walls were covered in bugs and from the ceiling they were dropping in clumps of thousands onto the floor. Horrified, I looked at my body, I too was covered in bugs; the room swirled around me as though in a Hitchcock thriller. I then did as any eight-year old child is entitled to do; I freaked out and ran screaming out of the hen house!

Frantically, I ran up the hill while scraping at my head and arms. Mom came out to the porch to see what the hollering was all about. She saw me heading her way and immediately pointed to the basement door, "don't come near the house," she hollered. Mom never did well with germs or creepy crawlies. She came down to the basement, keeping a five-foot distance, and instructed me to remove my clothes and get in the shower. The warm water beat down on me. I gagged while choking back the tears, and hysterically shampooed my hair and scrubbed my skin raw.

During the next few days, my father washed down the walls with a chemical to rid the coop of the pesky critters. Meanwhile, the eggs continued to gather for they had not been collected. Mom said, one night over dinner, "Aubri, I want you to collect the eggs after school tomorrow." Apprehensively, I agreed to her request while swallowing down another bite of beans, ugh!

So, the following day… It was another adventure in the hen house…

Big Red

Cautiously, I approached the chicken coop, basket in hand. I stood there for a moment before touching anything. Peering in, I searched the ceiling, walls and chickens. I didn't see anything unusual or feel anything creepy. *I guess it's all right*, I said to myself, while carefully I scrutinized each egg, before placing it in the basket.

There sat Big Red, perched high in her nest as she rested. I approached with quiet caution. *I'll just reach under her carefully. I don't want to frighten her.* Holding my breath, I gently slid my hand under the warm red-feathered hen, when suddenly, she woke up; and nearly instantly, I had a wild chicken on my hands. Squawking loudly, she savagely pecked the top of my hand and blood oozed out. I ran in the direction of the gate as she chased after me. I managed to break free. I still could hear her angry protests as I fled from the barn.

That evening at the dinner table, Mom asked in front of the whole family why I had not collected the eggs.

All eyes were upon me as I nervously explained in detail what had happened. I held my red swollen hand up for my Mom to see.

"But, the eggs will spoil. You need to collect them tomorrow after school."

"But, I'm afraid to."

Dad spoke, and we always listened when he spoke. "Aubrianna Rose, you do as your mother says. You collect tomorrow's eggs, or you'll be punished.

You just need to show the chickens whose boss!" he encouraged.

The following day in school, I tried not to think about angry Big Red. When I got home, I went about my chores, saving the obvious egg collecting for last. I retrieved my little red basket, and approached the chicken coop. The warm inviting barn did not stave off my frightened feelings, my father's belt was more to be feared than Big Red. Breathing deeply, I thought, *just think of yourself as Clint Eastwood*. The classic music played in the background, I adjusted my holster, my metal stirrups scraped the old wooden floor boards, as I approached the "coop saloon." The barn doors were pushed open with an Eastwood confidence, as I began collecting the eggs, and saving Big Red for last.

There she was perched high in her nest, keeping her eggs warm. As I approached, she became agitated. Slowly and cautiously, I walked toward her. My cool, steady, calculating gaze met hers as I set the basket on the ledge beside her. Her agitation escalated the closer I got. My Clint Eastwood nerves of steel quickly diminished. The fear of Dad's belt made me realize I had no choice. I spoke, "You can do this!" While reaching under her to gather the eggs, she loudly protested and pecked my hand hard, the scabs were reopened on the top of my swollen hand, blood oozed again. She continued pecking the top of my hand, when a warm shock wave crossed over me. The other chickens nervously paced the hen house, not pleased with the egg stealing thief.

For one brief moment, I panicked. However, I knew I had to win or else! I surprised myself when suddenly I grabbed Big Red up by the neck with one hand and quickly filled the basket with the other. Adrenaline coursed through my body. I couldn't believe, I had the courage to do it; Big Red was equally surprised. She looked dazed and shook her head in disbelief. I left the chicken coop, adjusted my cowboy hat, and held my head high as I proudly walked up the hill with my basket of eggs.

The following day, I approached Big Red with basket in hand. Her steely eyes watched me. I reached for her neck, when much to my surprise, she lifted her red feathered fanny, so I could gather her eggs. So, the battle for farm fresh eggs, was finally over! "Hmmm, maybe I should have tried the Clint Eastwood technique, on the stubborn pony Shorty, "Nah, its best to leave that one alone".

Creek Fort

One of my favorite places was our creek at the bottom of the hill. One cold rainy winter, our creek became a raging river and swelled with an awe-inspiring force. She pushed the waters forward in a thunderous, unbridled motion and carved away the river bank. A Redwood tree was uprooted from the storm.

During summer, the fallen tree made a perfect tree fort. The tree lay on its side in the sand alongside the now gentle brook. The roots were splayed out like a giant spider—just the spot to hang brightly colored kitchen towels, tins filled with ginger and cinnamon spices, and precariously perched colored glass bottles. In the sunlight, the glass bottles glowed of amber, blue and green. We also had what all forts should have, snacks, snacks, and more snacks!

Most summer days you'd find me in the creek. I couldn't run to my enchanted creek fast enough. On warm days, I'd roll my pant legs far above my knees, wade in the water and search for specks of Fool's Gold or little gem stones. Some days, I'd ditch Luke, so I could enjoy the magic on my own—lying stretched out on the sand and lulled by nature's mesmerizing beauty; feeling the warm sun on my skin was comforting. The creek was a sacred place to me.

Free Me From My Cage

It's Polliwog Time

I'll remember those days with special fondness. The warm, slimy water between my toes, while cautiously wading through the water, and avoiding slippery stones. For two youngsters, what came next became a ceremonial experience—for instance, not just any container would do. Down into the basement Luke and I ran in search of the "perfect jar." The room was cool and dimly lit.

The ceiling creaked above us as Mom cooked in the kitchen, which added more thrill and excitement as we whispered and tiptoed about, trying to muffle our squeaks of enthusiasm. We approached the canning shelf where Mom stored her summer harvest of fetching colors: Mason jars filled with tomatoes, corn, red peppers, green beans, and one of our favorites, apple sauce.

Vigilantly, we scanned the shelf, and there it was—the biggest glass pickle jar I ever laid eyes on! It sat proudly on the top shelf as though wearing a blue ribbon. It beckoned my eager young hands. I stood on my tippy toes and stretched up as far as I could. My fingers touched the cool glass. As I scooped it off the shelf edge, it came down so fast I almost lost it, but I quickly rescued it from a near shattering death. "Phew, that was a close one," I whispered to Luke. Now that we had the perfect jar, we couldn't get out of the basement and into the bright sunny outdoors quick enough. Luke and I ran giggling to the creek, with the large pickle jar tucked safely under my arm.

We found the perfect place. The creek spilled gently over mossy covered rocks, forming a shallow water hole. The sun shimmered brightly off the water, allowing us to catch sight of those exciting little creatures. We couldn't be bothered with rolling up our pant legs; after all, half our fun was getting wet and muddy! The water went half way between our ankles and knees. We snickered as warm muddy water oozed between our toes. Squealing with laughter, we watched those little squirmies, darting around our feet and disappearing quickly.

We carefully placed the pickle jar on its side in the water, disguised with mud, slime and pebbles. We held our breath with nervous anticipation as we waited for the future frogs to enter their glass home. This agonizingly slow technique eventually paid off. Leaving the creek, we walked up the hill with weighted down pant legs, weeds and dried grass were stuck to our muddy bare feet, and water slopped over the rim of our pickle jar. We smiled proudly as we exchanged stories of who caught the biggest polliwog.

Our next challenge was finding a hiding spot Mom wouldn't discover! We'd be in big trouble if she found them and then we would have to take them back to the creek. So, where do we hide them? "Under the bed?" Luke asked. "I know, I know, how about mama's canning shelf? The closet?" he asked sheepishly, while running out of five-year old suggestions.

"No little Luke, Mom would find 'um." The only safe place was the basement window sill. *"It should be high enough, surely she wouldn't find it there,"* I silently hoped.

The following day, I heard mom yelling my name loudly from the basement. "Aubri Rose! I ran to the basement, skidding to a halt. With surprise, I saw Mom holding the jar away from her body as though the slimy toothless critters would jump out and bite her. No words were needed; I knew what I must do. So off I went with slumped shoulders and freed the polliwogs from their cramped glass home.

To this day, I never discourage my sons from catching and bringing home polliwogs, crawdads, turtles, lizards, snakes, or any other critters. Although, I draw the line with skunks. It is all a part of our curious nature, which in my opinion should never be squelched. I still love the memories of walking hand in hand with my sons. Holding our nets and buckets, while walking in the direction of our nearest creek, in search of those still exciting little creatures. Every summer, my water fountains are flooded with polliwogs as we watch the still exciting transformation ... we had frogs, lots and lots of frogs!

Parents, please have fun with your children— enjoy the little things in life, they prove to be the most rewarding.

Abandoned School House

One cool breezy day in Fall, I sat beneath a Monterey Cypress, upon its gnarled and exposed roots with tufts of willowy grass growing between them. The stately, majestic trees separated our property line from our neighbor Mr. Bubbles and the abandoned school house. I leaned my head back against the rough trunk and stared high into the lofty branches. From time to time, the ominous school house whispered to me, distracting my gaze and sending chills down my spine.

Why does it call to me? Reaching down, I pulled a single blade of grass from the clump growing beside me, when I felt the tickling sensation run down my spine again, the old structure whispered to me a second time.

I stood and began walking in its direction. Not having the company of my sister Susan made it scarier. She and I often pretended to be Nancy Drew; the thrill of solving mysteries was so exciting. I strolled through the overgrown meadow, which was a former baseball field.

A cool breeze gently touched my face as I approached the play area. A melancholy feeling swept over me as I heard distant laughter of children from days gone by. And now, a lonely playground void of joyous squeals. Standing before me was a tall, rusty slide; and to the right was an old gigantic merry-go-round. I walked to the swing set, and gently sat upon the old weathered, yet sturdy seat. Holding onto the chains, I began to swing my legs. She creaked, moaned and sighed as her kinks gradually broke free.

In a short time, the lonely playground no longer frightened me. The playground's Motherly memories were reawakened by the laughter of children again. Whenever Ben, Susan, Liz, Luke and me ran across the Monterey Cypress property line, we always brought our own sheets of wax paper for a guaranteed fast ride down the slide.

Climbing aboard the merry-go-round was especially thrilling. Ben had us all pile on and hold tightly, while he pushed with all his might, he'd jump aboard when he pushed fast enough. Our smiling faces were red and radiant as we squealed loudly. Even Merry herself managed a rusty smile of satisfaction, as her steel, motherly arms reached circularly around her happy children once again.

My mind drifted as I swung in and out of the future; back and forth under the swing's hypnotic distraction. Remembering once again my goal, Nancy Drew hopped off the swing and headed straight to the abandoned school house alone. Making my way to the building's side entrance, I stepped up to a large paned window with faded chipped white paint around the wooden frame. On tippy toes, I Hesitated slightly before peering in. The rooms were spacious with hardwood flooring. I was surprised to see sofas rather than desks and chalk boards. My detective skills later discovered an immigrant Mexican family lived there temporarily while working in the apple fields.

It didn't take me long to befriend my extended family, regardless of our language barrier. The young married couple had a toddler boy, usually wearing nothing but a diaper. I grew most fond of the smiling elderly woman always wearing a pretty dress with an apron tied to her waist.

One room was converted into a makeshift kitchen. Baskets hung from the ceiling filled with tomatoes, onions, red chili peppers and garlic, lots and lots of garlic. The counter space displayed brightly colored yellow, blue and green mixing bowls, nestled neatly on top of each other, along with sacks of flour, cornmeal, rice, and beans. An antique stove had large cast iron pots filled with rich bubbling molé sauce, chili beans, and rice. The large picture window was almost always covered in steam with delicious aromas baking inside.

One day after school, I casually strolled through the playground, when off in the distance, I saw the father chasing after a chicken with an ax in his hand. Not wanting to see or hear what came next, I ran straight to the school house and into the kitchen. The elderly woman was frying flour tortillas; the smell was heavenly. She removed a hot tortilla from the skillet, spread it with butter, and sprinkled it with salt. She rolled it up and handed it to me.

"For me?" I asked surprised, for she hadn't done that before.

"Si," she said.

That was the best tortilla I'd ever had, and I was grateful she didn't put chicken in it!

Indians

"I'm an Indian and I was born in a teepee," I would tell my friends. When I first learned of the Natives, I was fascinated by them. Sometimes I would pretend to be an Indian gathering acorn's off the ground, then placing them in patches of sunlight. The following day, I gathered the acorns and placed them on a large flat stone. The fun began! I hit them hard with another rock just like they did in the movie I'd watched in school. My goal was to make a corn flour. What I made was a mess. However, it was fun.

My third-grade teacher, Mrs. Purtle, had given me and my fellow classmates a book assignment on Indians. I was assigned to research the Santa Barbra Tribe of Southern California. The more I read of the Indians, the more I wanted to be one. And little did I know, on Grandmas next visit what thrilling news I would discover!

Grandma's Shocking News

One of Grandma's visits was most memorable. After dinner, Grandma and I went into the living room. I wanted to keep her company because she was alone. I wasn't sure what to talk about, so I decided to tell her about my 3rd grade class. Then, I told her about my book report on Indians; I was surprised to see she gave me her full attention. Quickly, I rattled off as much information as I could while I had her attention. Her eyes watched me as she listened to every word. Eventually, I had exhausted my supply of Indian knowledge.

Grandma spoke, "Aubri?"

"Yeah, Grandma?"

"Did you know you have Indian in you?"

I sputtered in disbelief, "What, Grandma?"

"You have the Black Foot tribe in your bloodline."

"I'm an Indian? Really, Grandma? I'm an Indian?" I shouted out loud!

"Yes, you're part Indian. My father was Blackfoot Indian, and my Grandfather was a Blackfoot Chief. It wasn't talked about back when I was just a girl. It wasn't considered something to be proud of I was not happy to hear I had a Native Father, I never wanted to see him, I screamed at him one day when I got off the train to meet him, I yelled at him, you're not my Father, and ran away from him. I was your age Aubri." She reflected and paused while recalling her child hood memory.

"Really, but why would you treat your father that way? The Indians were nature people? Oh, my goodness I can't believe I'm an Indian, I'm so happy Grandma, I'm so happy!" I smiled proudly.

Ben and the rest of the gang came into the living room to investigate my enthusiasm. "Grandma says we're Indian," I explained. My brothers and sisters didn't share my enthusiasm. Their reaction was more like being told, "Hey kids, we're having beans for dinner tonight."

Everyone believed my love of Indians was only the passing phase of an eight-year old. The following day, I floated into school, my head held high as though I were born of nobility. If Big Red had let me yank a tail feather from her back side, I would have gladly worn it in my hair.

Chapter Five
The Last of My Father's Rages!

One evening, Mom and Dad went out for dinner and a movie, leaving Ben in charge. The delicious smell of buttered popcorn filled the house. I sat on the big comfy green sofa curled up close to Ben. We stuffed handfuls of warm salted popcorn into our mouths. My eyes were glued to the TV as we watched a scary show called *Night Gallery.* The eerie music held me captive! A woman peered down a dimly lit hallway wearing nothing but a white cotton night shirt. In her trembling hand, she held a flickering candle. Cautiously, she moved forward, as the music intensified!

My attention was drawn away from the television by high pitched squeals of laughter coming from my bedroom. Relieved by the distraction, I cheerfully scooted off the couch to investigate the joyful sounds. My two older sisters Susan and Liz were both jumping on my bed. This should have been the time for me to speak up saying, "Hey, you guys jump on your own beds!"

Their faces radiated joy as they jumped up and landed on their butts. "Come on Aubri, you try it," they giggled.

"But we're not supposed to jump on the beds," I replied.

"Ahhh, come on," they whined!

With slight hesitation I agreed, "Well, okay, but just this once."

They bounced off and onto the floor. I scrambled up onto my bed, took a deep breath, jumped high and landed on my butt. We heard a cracking sound as my mattress suddenly went crooked.

My sisters' smiling faces froze. "You're going to be in trouble when Dad gets home."

Ben rushed in shaking his head, "Oh man, this isn't good." (No doubt concerned what Dad would also do to him, since he was in charge.)

Later that night, I crawled into my lopsided bed. Comments my sisters had made echoed in my head, *"You're gonna be in trouble when dad gets home."* Tears ran down my cheeks. My stomach felt queasy. Fear took over my thoughts. Nervously, I devised a plan to suffocate myself. In the mind of an eight-year-old, death would be easier than being whipped with Dad's belt! I placed the pillow over my face and took a deep breath! Roughly twenty seconds passed, I gasped for air, trying a second and third time. Several attempts later, my lungs burned, and my head reeled with pressure. I ripped the pillow from my face and cried myself to sleep.

At about 11:30PM, our bedroom light switched on, awakening me from a deep sleep. I lifted my head from the tear-soaked pillow and squinted through tired eyes at my Dad standing over me. He looked at the crooked bed and yelled for me to get up. Terrified, I scrambled out of bed and onto the floor. He ordered me to pull down my pajama bottoms. (That was always very humiliating.) He demanded, "Bend over your bed."

"Daddy, please don't," I begged.

I heard metal clanking behind me as he removed his belt. Nervously, I shook within. I held my breath, and squeezed my eyes tightly shut. The first impact of leather against my bare skin sent shock waves through me. He yelled, "Haven't I told you not to jump on the bed?" The striking belt cut through my skin again, and again. He left the room in a rage. I collapsed to the floor sobbing; no one came to comfort me.

Hide It!

I was nearly twelve years old, with the memory I'm about to share. One summer evening, my family and I attended our weekly Bible study. A group of fifteen to twenty members gathered in a friend's home. My Dad facilitated the group study. One man, generally an elder, read a paragraph, and Dad asked questions from the material read. People raised their hands, as in school. We waited to be called on by my Dad and answered the question. To please my Dad, we needed to regularly raise our hand; his children were to set a proper example! The topic that night was the beasts of Revelation! How could an eleven-year-old (that would be me) share in that discussion when the adults had difficulty comprehending it?

That evening, I sat beside my sister Liz; she often whispered the answer to a question in my ear. She was smart and rarely wrong, which helped me feel confident when raising my hand.

Luke was sitting on the other side of Liz drawing pictures with a pencil. He decided he wanted Liz's bright green felt pen and attempted to grab it! I was oblivious to Luke's annoying antics! Dad asked a question to the group regarding one of the Beasts of Revelation rising out of the sea—what world power did it represent? Liz leaned over placing her green pen in my lap and whispered, "Hide it!" I thought she was giving me the answer to the question. So straight up in the air went my hand with a gleam in my eye. *Dad will be so proud of me*, I hoped. Seeing my enthusiastic expression, he called out, "Aubrianna." With no thought what so ever, I proudly blurted out, "Hide it."

Everyone roared with laughter. *Oh, my goodness, what did I say wrong?* I worried. My cheeks flushed with warmth! Liz elbowed me hard while she whispered, "The felt pen, I wanted you to hide it!" My body went limp with fear. I looked at Dad and saw the masked anger on his face! He attempted to laugh it off with the rest; however, I saw his eyes and they were not smiling.

In the car on our way home, my Dad told Liz and me we would not have dessert as our punishment. We were greatly relieved not to get beat with the belt! However, we were disappointed not to have Mom's delicious pineapple upside down cake and vanilla ice cream. How could we forget, the house smelled incredible, she had pulled it out of the oven minutes before we left for bible study.

Liz and I were told we would be sleeping in the outdoors tank house. I was relieved we'd be outside away from Dad's anger.

In my cotton night dress, I put clean sheets on my bed. Meanwhile Liz was obviously annoyed with my accidental blunder. "It's all your fault we're not getting dessert Aubri! I can't believe you said that! I wasn't giving you an answer. I wanted you to hide the pen, I shouldn't have to miss out on dessert Aubri, its all your fault! Liz was absolutely right, she should not have had to miss out on dessert. I shouldn't have either for that matter, my Dads pride was humiliated from my innocent mistake, he took it far to personal when people laughed.

Not wanting to cause any more problems, I told her again and again, how sorry I was. However, her annoyance continued. So, I attempted ignoring her insults, by paying extra attention to smoothing out the wrinkles in my sheets. This clearly was not a good idea. My gesture made her more upset! Her insults continued to fly! Until... As the infamous cartoon character Popeye said, "That's it. I can't stanz it no more!" A can of spinach was not needed. This was a verbal war! I firmly blurted out, "Shut up and leave me alone, Liz!"

Liz's expression changed, when Dad entered the open door behind me. The color drained from my face as I turned around in shock and disbelief, for I knew he had heard me tell Liz to shut up and leave me alone. He angrily went through the motion of loosening his belt as he yanked and tugged! "Aubri, get over here," he barked! (I realize as I write this today my father was enraged with humiliation from my wrong answer at the Bible study; he simply used that opportunity to beat me!)

What happened next, was my first connection with a foreign part within myself. My inner warrior, a primal instinctual part of me. Because of his seething anger, he was unable to get his belt free from its loops. I knew it was only a matter of time before he would free it and unleash his anger on me. It was at that exact moment I ran straight past him and outside! The breeze gently caressed my hot panic-stricken face, my heart beat a terrifying rhythm. The air smelled of freshly mowed lawn and the scent of apples lingered in the cool night air.

However, nature's innocence didn't calm my shock, and I had no plan of where to go. Wildly, I searched for a place to hide. I could only think of Mom; I ran feverishly across the stepping stones towards the back steps which lead to the kitchen. Even though my Mom had never saved me from dad's wrath before, I still ran to her out of instinct. Dad's rage escalated! (For he had now and for the first time, lost his control over me.) He yelled out my name and grabbed the wooden-handled broom beside the door and ran after me. My attempt to outrun him was futile. Now only inches away, he swung the wooden handle into my back with all his wrath. I screamed out a blood curdling scream, the pain was unbelievably disturbing. He repeated the blows into my back with a vengeance; the pain seared through my skin as though I was being cut with a knife. Wildly, my mind and spirit left my body, the pain was more than I could endure. However, my body still went through the motions of completing my mission.

I ran up the stairs and into the kitchen when suddenly, from behind, he grabbed a fist full of my hair, and pulled me back to him. With his free hand, he grabbed my shoulder and turned me around to face his rage. I lost control of my bladder and urine poured down my legs. I stood bare foot in a puddle of urine. His fist still held tightly to my hair as he lifted me up off the floor, and inches away from his horrifying face! "I better never hear you say, shut up again. Do you hear me? Now clean up this mess or I'll clean it up with your hair!" He set me back down on trembling legs. I gasped for air in between sobs. My head felt as though it were bleeding from hair being ripped out. I trembled in shock as he repeated his barking command, "Don't ever say that again, do you hear me?"

"Yes," I feebly said,

I cleaned the urine off the floor and went straight to bed. Silently, I wept with no one to console me. No opportunity was given for me to explain myself. I learned early on to silence my voice, or I suffered more severely!

That Summer evening, was the last of my Father's rage. He never struck me again. Perhaps he realized he'd gone over the edge and lost control that night.

Free Me From My Cage

Welcome to Healdsburg

Chapter Six

Healdsburg

When I was twelve, my Dad moved his family of seven again. Our new home was in Healdsburg, California. Healdsburg was, and still is an upscale town. Healdsburg is surrounded by beautifully landscaped vineyards, and the town center is my favorite. Redwood trees and lush green lawn grace the Main Street square. Quaint shops and elegant restaurants surround the town park on all four sides. Once a week, the traffic is re-routed for a wine in the park festival featuring live music, dance, food, beer, and wine.

Our home was a large ranch style house with sprawling front and back lawns. We had a distant, yet dramatic view of Mt. St. Helena. One side of our home had an enormous patio with a built-in covered barbeque pit, an ideal place for knee slapping' square dance parties. Off the patio was a door leading into the house through the pantry, which became stocked with enough food to feed several armies, (a tad bit of exaggeration.) My religion taught that the year 1975 would be the Great Tribulation, the Second Coming. Therefore, my parents began stockpiling food one year before the prophesied event. Having this constant threat of Armageddon hanging over my head held me mentally captive in a constant state of terror.

Down the hallway and past the pantry was an outrageously huge walk-in freezer, large enough for two cows, maybe even three, (not an exaggeration.) The guest bathroom had a spacious shower that would comfortably hold six people. It had impressive glass shower doors, etched with lovely mermaids. There was a staff kitchen and laundry room. We could enter the main kitchen from the laundry room through a large swinging door, the kind you'd see in restaurants separating the kitchen from the dining room. It had a shiny, polished silver plate instead of a door knob; one hardy push would swing the door open into the main family kitchen. Our kitchen, like the rest of the house, was larger than most homes, with counter space and cabinets galore. We ate breakfasts in the kitchen and evening meals in the dining area. I never really understood the purpose of needing two eating areas.

Our living room had a fireplace with a built-in rock bench. Large picture windows filled every room of the house. Funny thing though; with all those windows, the house still seemed dark to me. (I'll fill you in on that one later.) The dining and living area had French doors opening to an outdoor private balcony that overlooked an amazing ancient oak and sweeping vineyard views. From the dining room and front entry way of our home was a long hallway leading to three bedrooms and the family bathroom.

My sister Liz and I shared a room next to mom and dad. It was the smallest room in the house. My baby sister Anne and Luke also shared a room. Susan's bed room was at the far end of the house by the second kitchen and laundry area. My brother Ben was now married. He and his wife got the guest cabin located at the end of our driveway, just past the row of cedar trees. His home needed a major renovation; in time, dad converted it into a charming honeymoon cottage.

We were fortunate enough to have a swimming pool for staving off the sweltering heat of long summer days. However, it was not your average pool. As was everything else, it was enormous! We called it our Olympic pool. In fact, we wondered if at one time it was open to the public because of the large rusted metal signs which hung in various areas stating the rules: No running! No pushing! No urinating! We also had an outdoor shower, a wading pool for toddlers, and a large built-in bench which appeared long enough to seat twenty or more.

Would you believe, running through our backyard, was another creek? Unlike our creek in Sebastopol which ran year-round, this creek merely trickled. It also had blackberry bushes roaming wild and free with a mission statement I believe all blackberries seem to have: *Go ahead and cut us down, but we'll be back!* A stepping stone path led to our pump house down the hill, near the trickling creek. As I mentioned earlier, summers were hot in Healdsburg. Consequently, our well often went dry, which meant the pump needed to be shut off, so it wouldn't overheat. That was my job. When I heard Mom's nervous, high pitched call, "Aubri Rose, the well went dry!" I'd scramble quickly to the bottom of the hill.

I entered the cinderblock pump house which smelled of oil, dirt and sunbaked bricks. The overheating pump emitted a hot engine odor. The pump stood taller than me and vibrated loudly, sounding as though metal was clanking against metal. Holding my breath, I cautiously reached for the switch, fearful of touching the radiating heat for surely, I thought, my skin would melt into it. When it was switched off, the metal monster came to a shaking halt! And so, did I.

Having very little water during the summer months proved challenging for my brothers and sisters. We had two choices for washing our hair. We could either crawl under the fence to our neighbor's tractor storage barn and use their faucet (for teenage girls that was extremely embarrassing, especially if caught by the guys laboring in the vineyards), or we could jump into our pool for a memorable shampoo and cream rinse experience.

Elementary School

Luke, Annie, and I attended Westside Elementary, a charming little school down a country road about two miles from our home. The small school offered me a temporary place of calm. Mr. Dennis was my sixth-grade teacher. He was a tall, slim man in his late fifties with gray hair. He wore thick prescription glasses, which made his eyes resemble an owl's. He loved telling us stories of his past rather than the subject matter in our textbooks, which of course was always welcomed by his students.

Soon, I graduated from the sixth grade. My parents were faced with the choice of placing me in two junior high schools. Because we lived so far out in the country, my parents opted for Windsor rather than Healdsburg. Unknowingly, my parents put me in a school that caused me additional pain. Even though I'm not a racist person, and I will repeat those words: I'm not a racist person, I found myself in a school where I was in the minority. It was populated mostly with Mexican-Americans who didn't take a liking to us whities.

Blanca Bitch

My slim curvy frame and blue green eyes, with waist length golden hair made me a target for trouble. The girls were jealous because their men (boys) were attracted to me. Little did they know, I was sooo not into boys yet.

Every day at school was a new challenge, and one day in particular stands out. I sat in a warm patch of sunlight eating a juicy orange and sunflower seeds. I talked with my girlfriend Brenda about the Bible, when I noticed what appeared to be trouble headed our way. Three girls approached me; the one in the middle was enormous and muscular while the two girls on each side of her were thin, however their tough attitudes made up for it. Their stride had trouble written all over it and I knew I couldn't make it to the office in time for shelter. Nervously, I watched the potential trouble approaching. The over-sized girl barked out in her broken English,

"Stand up, Blanca bitch!"

Still sitting, I calmly spoke, "I don't want to fight."

She barked again, "Get up."

I was a strong girl despite my slim build; however, I knew my limitation and she stood growling before me. A familiar knot formed in the pit of my stomach. Slowly, I stood, my inner wisdom spoke, *whatever happens, don't hit her back*. I spoke to her calmly, "I don't want to fight." My stomach tightened because I knew what was going to happen.

She made a fist that went straight for my face, connecting a hard strike! Her angry eyes held a fleeting expression of sadness, as they switched to anger again. Much to my surprise, she didn't strike a second time. She left with her friends.

One day, I stood in my gym class line before the teacher had arrived. Roughly twenty girls were in the auditorium, high pitched squeals echoed around me. I felt self-conscious in my blue wrinkled jumpsuit, that I'd yanked from my locker just minutes before. My desire was to disappear into a crevice in the wall, far away from these girls speaking a rapid language I did not understand.

Painfully, I was forced back into harsh reality by a handful of my hair being maliciously pulled from behind. Girls wailed with laughter while pointing at me. Humiliated, I told her to leave me alone. Her malicious antics were fueled by the other girls, which caused her to yank and rip at my hair even harder. She bellowed out, "What do you think of that, white bitch? You think you're so much better than us, huh? You better stay away from my boyfriend."

"I don't want your boyfriend or anyone else's," I responded.

She shoved me hard into a girl standing beside me, nearly knocking us both to the ground. The room exploded with laughter and excitement while they surrounded me just as guys do when ready to watch a fight. I was faced with two options: either run out of the room defeated, or fight! Having a peaceful nature, the thought of fighting went against my better judgment. Yet something primitive within me stirred, and like a tiger I pounced on her, and grabbed a handful of her hair at the nape of her neck and twisted it around my fist as though wringing out a wet rag. She screamed for me to let go. All eyes were upon me, the students were silent! I spoke firmly and loud enough for the others to hear, "Don't you ever touch me again." I tightened my grip one final twist before letting go.

The office staff was fully aware of my mistreatment because I went to the office for shelter nearly every day. They called my parents, encouraging them to consider transferring me to a different school. Unfortunately, my parents never shared their concerns.

After school, we were stuffed like sardines into a large school bus. My bus ride was nearly an hour's ride home. One day, the bus came to a tired, groaning halt at the bottom of my driveway. The bus driver walked me across the road as usual; however, this time I was surprised because she spoke to me. "Aubrianna, I want you to know how impressed I am with you. These kids treat you terribly and you just keep taking it. I understand you're one of Jehovah's Witnesses, I'd like you to teach the Bible to my daughter, Dorothy. She attends Healdsburg Junior High. I think you girls will get along well."

I was surprised to be having a conversation with the bus driver and I was equally surprised that she was aware of my mistreatment. Later that evening, she called my parents and told them how I'm treated on the bus. She told them about the school in Healdsburg. I had nearly completed seventh grade. However, I was grateful to finish at Healdsburg Junior High. And though it had its own challenges, they paled in comparison, (pun intended.)

As I recall these few memories I've shared, it saddens me that family life becomes so hectic that the pleas of our bullied children go unheard. Mothers and fathers, I lovingly urge you to listen to your children or young adults. Look into their eyes and see the burdens they carry from school bullies. And do something about it!

Cruel Labels

In high school, the "retarded ones" underwent cruel and senseless treatment from bullying teenagers. Anyone appearing unique did not fit into the bullies' box of "normal standards." Having an understanding, and relating to their pain, I compassionately reached out to them as though a mother hen, (not "Big Red") and safely tucked them under my wing. My children were the emotionally challenged, the overweight, the unattractive, the buck-toothed kids with speech impediments, and so on. Me their surrogate mother, now wore a new label: the "Holy Roller Nerd Girl."

During my freshman year, I walked down a long corridor with my friend Dorothy (her mother was the school bus driver.). We walked past three smirking Jehovah's Witness girls. Their arms were folded while they leaned against the wall and looked at me with disgust—yes, you heard me right, three of my alleged spiritual sisters. They banned together and pushed over a large metal garbage can. It crashed loudly to the floor and echoed down the hall. They picked up apple cores, half-eaten sandwiches, and whatever disgusting garbage they could find to throw at Dorothy and me. Their laughter echoed down the hall as they yelled from behind, "Christian of the year! Christian of the year!" Needless to say, I was mortified, yet held my composure and kept walking.

Not Fitting In

Home life continued to be challenging. Dad's raging temper still sent riveting shock waves through me. Although one day things dramatically shifted: Dad survived his first heart attack in his early forties. The first few months, Mom said more than anything else, "Sshh! Be quiet! your father's sleeping!"

When I'd come home after another challenging day of school, I wished my mother had been the sort I could discuss my problems with, one of which was feeling like the family work horse. She had a list of chores for me, as did my Dad. Some of my chores were more suitable for a man rather than a young girl.

I no longer got along with my sisters which deeply hurt and confused me; I didn't know why they would shut me out. I remember leaving notes on their pillows asking them why they wouldn't talk with me, telling them I was sorry for whatever I'd done wrong, and that I loved them.

At fourteen years of age, my hair was long and thick. When I washed my hair, I was unable to comb through the tangles. So, my mother volunteered my sisters to comb it out. I don't blame them for being annoyed; it took them both close to an hour, as they took turns ripping through my hair.

However, I eventually tired of the grueling, painful routine, as I'm sure my sisters did also. So, I opted to have my hair cut short at the age of fifteen. The hair dresser gently gathered my hair together and asked, "Are you having second thoughts? It's not too late to change your mind." I think he was more nervous than me. I can still hear the sound as he cut through thick layers of my hair. I walked away with the new rage in hair styles: the Dorothy Hamilton hairdo.

Saving Grace

One day, my chore was to mow (the mower was a lot larger than an ordinary mower) the back hillside and to mow in and around the pine trees. On day two, I was having difficulty pushing the mower up the steep portion of the hill, so I tried getting a running start. I continued that pace until nearly passing out from exhaustion. My next attempt was, pulling it inch by inch up the hill, while breathing in the smelly puffs of black smoke that smelled of burnt oil. I grunted as beads of sweat dripped down my forehead while pulling the red metal monster up the steep hill. Then suddenly I slipped on the grass: my left leg shot out from underneath me and right into the spinning blades of the lawn mower! I squeezed my eyes tightly shut, expecting my foot to be severely cut. The blade made a loud noise as it hit the rubber of my tennis shoe, bringing the obnoxious motor to an immediate halt! The miraculous thing was: the day before when I was tackling the hill I was wearing my sandals! However, that morning, I couldn't find them, so I put on my Saving Grace tennis shoes instead!

My Best Friend Luke

During the summer months, I spent most my free time with Luke, he may have been my brother, however he was also my best friend. When our chores were completed for the day, I would look for Luke and off we'd go on our motorcycles through the vineyards and down the gradual sloping hills, to the Russian River. I felt free and alive as the wind blew wildly through my hair. We screamed with laughter and rode as fast as we had the nerve. Luke was much gutsier than I; he seemed fearless!

We swam in our pool nearly every summer day and competed in swimming races and watched to see who could make the biggest cannon ball splash!

Our favorite hideaway was the hayloft of our neighbor's barn. The rich overpowering smell of oat hay permeated our surroundings while we stepped over bat droppings and the remains of thousands of cricket legs—apparently, bats don't eat cricket legs. We would pounce into piles of hay. The stems poked into our bellies as we lay stretched out playing card games and reading comic books. Sometimes, we'd sneak our neighbor's fat whimpering puppies. We'd roll them up in our shirts, carefully climb the ladder to the loft, and release them into billowing piles, while we ooed and aahed at their adorable, chubby cuteness.

Diving Board Dance

One summer day when our parents were away, my sisters Luke and I decided to plug in our portable record player outside by the pool. We played the theme song from the movie *The Sting*, those two men Robert Redford and Paul Newman, were such dreamy hunks. We turned the volume up full blast and played that song over and over and over again. In our bathing suits, we lined up on the diving board and danced goofy dances, and whatever made us feel ridiculously silly! We would inch our way slowly to the edge of the board and jump off one at a time. We'd start the song over again, and our silly dances too. (We honestly must have played that song a hundred times that day.)

Those joyful childhood memories wash over me like a gentle spring rain: the pungent odor of oat hay in the dusty, cob-webbed loft; the warm, whimpering puppies; the breeze of freedom blowing through mine and Luke's hair; our swimming suits and skin smelling of chlorinated water the day we jitterbugged off the diving board.

Why Dark Feelings?

When I first wrote about the memories of our Healdsburg home, I realized the memories I shared with my readers are of what took place outside of our home. I never explained why the house seemed dark despite all the windows. I didn't want to discuss, remember, and especially not write about the memories that had haunted me. Terrifying nightmares trapped me in paralyzing fear, for decades, because of what transpired in our home. In fact, I speak on behalf of Susan, Luke, and my little sister Anne. Some things are just not meant to revisit; however, deep down, I felt the revisiting was necessary, which allowed me to face another past trauma fear. And in doing so, the demons were buried.

The house possessed a life of its own and its focus was primarily to terrify children. My first unexpected visit was on a cold and foggy autumn morning. The day before, I had checked out a book from the school library, it was filled with stories of mystery spots on the earth. I was fascinated with the topic and nearly completed the book within twenty-four hours. Because I had stayed up all night to finish the book, I had difficulty getting up for school the following morning. Mom told me to go ahead and stay home, while the rest of the gang went to school. Mom and my baby sister Anne left the house at 8:45 for preaching work.

The house was "empty", I relished the quiet solitude. Soon I was lulled into a warm and cozy sleep. Roughly an hour had passed, when I was awakened by my mother's voice. I distinctly heard my door swish open and her voice say, "Honey, I'm home." I wondered why she'd come back early as I raised my head from the pillow. Squinting through sleepy eyes, I was shocked to see no one standing before my open door! Then it felt as if something had jumped on top of me. I felt weighted down as though I were being pushed into the mattress. I was frozen in shock and unable to scream out God's name (Jehovah's Witnesses are taught to call upon the holy name when negative influences try to haunt us; they fear hearing it and leave.). Terrified, I wondered why this was happening to me. Silently, I pleaded over and over in my head, *Jehovah! Jehovah! Jehovah!*

Miraculously, the weight lifted, releasing its evil grip from my body and in one quick motion, the unseen presence left. My room felt strange as I lay shivering and horrified; I had never experienced anything like that before. Afraid to leave my bed, I pulled my blankets tightly under my chin, while I kept my eyes wide open. A few hours had passed, and I needed to relieve myself, but I still couldn't get out of bed. I was fearful the demon would get me if I walked down the hallway to the bathroom. So, I lay in bed terrified and shaking waiting for my mom to get home. She returned at 1:00 and was surprised to see I was still in bed. After using the bathroom, I explained to my Mom what had happened, however, she dismissed it as silly girl drama.

One evening around 9, Susan was sitting with her back turned to me at the dining room table. I snuck up behind her and whispered, "I've been watching you." Needless to say, I scared her. I felt bad for scaring her and apologized over and over again. A few minutes later, I went to the kitchen to have a piece of roast beef. I picked up the serrated knife and began slicing a piece, when I heard from behind me a deep masculine voice say, "I'm watching you!" Instantly, my skin was covered in a million goosebumps as I whirled around, still holding the knife, expecting to see Susan getting back at me. However, what I saw, was nothing!

My sister Susan was awakened out of her sleep, pulled out of her bed, and dragged across the floor! Luke said he was chased down the hallway by three or four savage dogs trying to attack him and then vanished instantly. Anne heard barking dogs that followed her around in different rooms of the house. She also said she heard her name being called out from the floor heater vents. And, one night, she was awakened from her sleep by a voice that whispered to her, "go outside and jump into the pool." Little Anne hadn't learned to swim yet.

My sister Liz and Mom were left alone from the evil pranks. Why that is, has always remained a mystery. My Dad wrote them off as silly dramatic stories, until one early morning around 3:00AM, he couldn't sleep. He left his bedroom and went into the living room and sat in his large green leather chair. He was touched by an unseen presence and wouldn't say anything else. Shortly after his "experience," he put the house on the market to sell.

Chapter Seven
Me, Pretty?

Being a sensitive child had its challenges. However, being abused and sensitive took on a whole different dynamic. My Dad teased us, however I honestly and without any hesitation know it was not malicious teasing. My Dad's only challenge was his horrible temper; however, he was an honorable down to earth man, he worked hard to provide for his family, and most definitely was a spiritual man. He took us camping regularly and taught us the wholesome enjoyments of life. So, back to what I said about Dads teasing: again, there was no maliciousness behind it, however, children take on the teasing as real. I believe the comments he made to my brothers and sisters had lasting effects on us. Whenever my Dad observed overweight people, he would make belittling comments. And if my sisters or I ever put on weight, he'd be quick to bring it to our attention. Mom was a perfectionist, which meant we never measured up to her high standards, and believe me, I do mean high standards, she quickly brought to our attention, any personal flaws! My brothers and sisters were in fact quite beautiful, however we all felt like ugly ducklings. We had absolutely no self-esteem! I'm sure Mom meant well, however my overly sensitive ways had me feeling the only way to meet her approval was if my appearance was perfect in her eyes.

I don't expect everyone to understand what I'm about to share. However, the horrific and unjustified discipline from my Dad did something to my thinking. Firstly, I held onto an accumulation of frustration, which should have been expressed. Secondly, what happens in the mind of an abused person is different for everyone. For me, I personally internalized everything. I often felt the need to fade away into the woodwork. And I found helping other people was a way of distracting me from my pain!

Each day of high school was challenging for me. One reason was, the boys disgusted me with their wagging tongues spouting remarks about my ample cleavage and their desire for having sex with me. A head cheerleader approached me one day; she asked if I'd join the team. She was met with a long pause while I blankly stared and wondered, *why would they want an ugly girl like me?* My awkward reply was, "Oh? Well, thanks for thinking of me, but I can't." Sadly, even if I'd had the confidence, my religion would not have allowed it. In fact, Jehovah's Witnesses were not allowed to join any sports teams in school. The reason was that it would take far too much of our time and eventually lead us astray.

Boys are So Cute

One day those strange creatures, miraculously shifted for me. Although, my standards were not for the crude rude boys. I'll never forget one guy in particular. His lack of vulgar ways set him way ahead of the rest, a kind and considerate guy. He played on the football team and his name was Gary Candoni. Oh, I forgot to mention another vital piece of information. He was tall, dark, and absolutely gorgeous! The girls went ga-ga crazy for Gary. It was not uncommon to hear his name mentioned among circles of giggling females, "Oh... Gary Candoni's sooo dreamy."

He and I had coed gym class together. I found myself looking forward to attending gym each day. Our teacher paired the two of us together in class. Whenever he would look at me to say something, all I saw were his kind, dreamy brown eyes. Needless to say, I had developed an enormous crush.

One afternoon, I was in the kitchen when I heard the phone ring. I answered with the usual hello? The voice on the other end was Gary Candoni! *Oh, my god!* My mind raced. *Did he call the wrong person?* "Hi Aubrianna, how's your summer going?"

"Ahhh, it's going good," I stammered out a shocked response. We talked small talk while my heart raced at a speed I hadn't experienced before.

A few minutes into our conversation, he asked, "I was wondering if I could take you to the Santa Rosa fair?"

Oh, my goodness, I panicked! (Our religion wouldn't let us date someone not of our faith and my father would have my neck in a sling if I were to say yes.) I desperately wanted to throw caution to the wind and blurt out, "YES! I'd love to, my beautiful knight in shining armor." Instead, he was met with a slight pause as I nervously contemplated my reply.

Gary asked, "Are you there, Aubrianna?"

"Yes, I'm here, it's just that, well you see, my father won't let me."

"Oh, well, okay then. I guess I'll see you in class?"

"Yes, of course. Thank you, Gary, for thinking of me." I hung up the phone, my head held low, as I whined, "It isn't fair... It just isn't fair... He's such a great guy."

As I traveled down memory lane with an innocent glimpse of my childhood crush, I became somewhat curious about Gary Candoni. So the Nancy Drew in me did a little research. He's married with children and is a retired Deputy Sheriff. He writes thriller mysteries with a twist. He incorporates a moral in his stories to teach and educate his readers in a spiritually uplifting way. Wow! Why does that not surprise me? What a guy... That Gary Candoni.

Pretty Boy

When I was fourteen, my family and I packed for a two-day Bible convention in Yuba City with roughly three thousand members in attendance. The main purpose in our congregating was spiritual enrichment and sharpening our Bible knowledge.

The convention center had an enormous cafeteria with seating for roughly four hundred. My Dad oversaw the beverage department and I was recruited to help. I would get up at the crack of dawn with Dad (the drill sergeant) while the rest of my family slept. We'd leave the hotel at 6:15AM and begin our prep work in the utility kitchen at 6:30. I learned how to brew a major amount of coffee for the morning breakfast crowd. I filled two large silver pitchers with coffee in one, and chilled orange juice in the other. By 7:00AM, hundreds of people filled the room, their trays loaded with glazed donuts, eggs and hash browns. As a server, I asked, "May I serve you coffee or juice?"

One couple stood out. A guy roughly nineteen or twenty was sitting with an older woman, possibly his mother. He wasn't dressed in his Sunday best as everyone else. He wore white painter's pants, a t-shirt, and a hat which read *Who the hell is Sam?* The woman sitting beside him looked a little embarrassed. I cheerfully smiled, asking him, "Coffee or juice?"

His grin made me feel awkward as he answered,
"Juice."

One Year Later

One year later, my family and I attended a seven-day Summer, Bible convention at the Santa Rosa fairgrounds. Roughly seven thousand followers came. Regardless of my feminine shyness, I was beginning to feel less awkward in my body. I loved the attention I received from the opposite sex. It excited me! I found I was attracted to young men versus boys.

On our intermission breaks, I walked around a bit and mingled with different friends. I saw a well-dressed young man hanging out with some guys. He gave a strange approving nod, as though he knew me. I later found out he was the guy from the cafeteria wearing the *Who the hell is Sam?* hat.

Another year had passed. I was sixteen years old. My family attended another Bible convention in Yuba City. While I walked around with my best friend Lisa on an intermission break, I felt a tickly sensation travel down my spine. I turned around to glance over my shoulder and there, in the distant crowd, was the young man, our eyes met, and he grinned, rather than smiled. The remainder of the day, on our breaks, the young man with the grin followed me at a distance. My girlfriends, including Susan and Liz, thought he was dreamy! His grooming was impeccable and his style of clothing equally matched. I was flattered the "pretty boy" seemed to take a liking to me.

The following day, my sister's friends and I were hanging out. I was surprised to see the "pretty boy" walking our way. He brazenly entered the arena of seven cackling hens. They circled him as though he were the last man on earth. I shyly kept my distance while admiring his obvious beauty. From time to time, he stared at me beyond the rows of girls encircling him. I felt an odd mixture of feelings I was unable to figure out. One was, *Oh, my god, I think he likes me*. And the other was the strange sensation each time he grinned. Regardless, I chose to ignore my first signs of inner guidance giving me a warning nudge! *No, No, No, He may be cute... BUT!*

My First Date

I no longer wanted to wear second hand clothes to school. My Mom was notorious for taking us to the Goodwill for all are clothing. In high school I decided I wanted to start buying clothes from the Codding Town mall. So, in the Summer five days a week, I picked prunes for Fopiano prune orchards at 6:00 AM. Till noon. The discouraging thing was, after a whole Summer of back breaking labor I had only earned enough to buy two pairs of pants, a sweater and two t-shirts. So, I started cleaning people's homes and working at the Healdsburg deli part time.

My Dad was chairman of our church clothing project. People donated beautiful clothing, some of it looked brand new. The clothing was for our brothers and sisters in Mexico. We kept them temporarily stored in my Dad's shop until delivery day. One afternoon, Mom said I could look through some of the items. "Maybe you'll find something that fits," she said. I found an adorable pair of green high heels which had long laces that wrapped all the way up my calves. They fit perfectly. I tilted my ankle from side to side admiring my find when mother's voice interrupted, calling loudly down the driveway, "Someone's on the phone for you, Aubri."

I answered the phone from in Dad's office. I felt a familiar feeling like I had when Gary Candoni called. "Pretty boy" was on the phone. Silently, I wondered if he was calling for one of my sisters, rather than me. He asked if I'd like to go roller skating. *Oh, my goodness, he's asking me out! Surely Dad would approve; after all, he's a Jehovah's Witness.* I told him that I first needed my Dad's approval.

That evening after dinner, I nervously asked Dad.

"You met him where?" his voice inquired.

"At last week's convention. He's a brother and he's twenty years old," I replied.

"Well," he contemplated, "I guess it'll be alright, you'll be taking your sisters as chaperones, though." "Okay," I excitedly replied.

One week later, Steve drove his perfectly washed and waxed black Porsche at a snail's pace down our long, winding gravel driveway. My Dad gave him the eye of scrutiny and asked where he's from.

"Napa Valley, I live in Calistoga."

My Dad then asked, "How long did it take you to get here?"

"About thirty-five minutes," Steve boasted.

Dad gruffly spoke, "Well, you must have driven like a bat out of hell. It should have taken you closer to an hour to get here. I better not hear you've been driving that fast with my daughters on board or it'll be the last time you see them, do you understand?"

Steve's reply of "yes" had a jagged edge to it.

When our date was over, he asked if we could go skating again. From that point forward, we saw each other every Wednesday night for roller skating, along with my sisters. Eventually, we gave up the skating and spent Saturday afternoons together. I enjoyed the time we had and soon realized I craved the attention he gave me. Within just a few weeks, he spoke of us getting married as if he'd proposed to me (which he hadn't.)

One day, after a usual grueling day of school, I faithfully did my chores and then prepared a celebration dinner. I made an enormous amount of lasagna and garlic bread along with a gigantic salad. Steve and his parents were coming to meet our family for the first time.

We had ten people seated at our dining room table. The evening was a success; everyone raved about my cooking abilities. Mom said, "Yes, Aubrianna is a good cook, we gave her the nick name of Betty Crocker." Now honey, why don't you go ahead and clear the table and start cleaning up the kitchen." I knew I had always done this; however, I thought possibly because I had prepared everything that I might have the night off from cleaning. My feelings were hurt while I tried not to cry.

Later that evening, while our parents sipped Scotch cocktails, Steve and I slipped outside to kiss beneath our peach trees. He asked me why my mother has me do so much work.

A lump formed in my throat and I told him I wasn't sure why. Then the tears started, "It just isn't fair," I cried, "I've always felt like her servant rather than her daughter."

"I'll take care of you," he assured me. "In fact, I'd prefer it if you didn't finish high school." Our religion taught Armageddon will come anytime soon, so the emphasis was not on education. I wanted to be rescued and Steve appeared to be my savior.

Little did I know, I should not have been dating, let alone considering marriage. I had absolutely no foundation to build a healthy relationship upon. I was a scared, confused and deeply wounded girl in a woman's body. My loving voice of wisdom spoke gently to me again, *Not a good idea... No, No, No.* Unfortunately, I was not able to think with clarity.

I Can't Marry You

Three weeks before Steve and I were to be married, my sisters and I went to a party. I enjoyed being there and seeing the happy smiling faces of my friends. We danced to *Shake Your Booty*, *Staying Alive* and my favorite, Gary Wright's *Dream Weaver*.

This was my first event since dating Steve where I was alone without him present. I felt more myself, contentedly happy, and giddy inside. My sister Susan came and stood beside me. With no hesitation, I blurted out, "I don't think I should marry Steve. Something just doesn't feel right."

She lowered her motherly voice, "Then don't! Something doesn't settle well with me either. Even Dad was surprised Steve wouldn't ask permission to marry you until two weeks ago. The only reason he did was because Dad confronted him on it."

"Yeah, I know. I'm just not sure I can tell him. I'm afraid, Susan."

Steve arrived late and when he walked into the room my body stiffened and my heart raced! I glanced nervously at Susan as Steve approached me.

She gave me a confident "you can do it" look as she walked away, allowing us privacy.

Steve sensed my demeanor had changed and asked, "What's wrong?" He had to pry for a while before I could gently lower the boom.

"I'm scared Steve, and I'm not sure we should get married."

He was silent for a moment and then he spoke in a tone I hadn't heard him use before, "If you don't marry me, I'll move far away from you. I won't tell you where I'm going and when you realize you've made a mistake, you will never be able to find me."

Oh, my goodness, I thought, *maybe I'm just suffering from the pre-wedding jitters everyone's been telling me about*. I dismissed my intuitive feelings and apologized for my behavior. His threat was not only controlling, it was mind manipulation. He Strategically, planted fear and doubt in my mind. Had I been a balanced healthy individual I would have recognized his divisive tactics.

Pre-Wedding Deception

Steve took great pride that I had not been with another man. He said he hadn't been in a sexual relationship either. "It's important that two people come together as virgins," he stated. Shortly after we married, he confessed that he had a summer love affair with a married woman and a sexual relationship with another girl after the affair. And he called himself a virgin? When someone lies to you that convincingly, it has you wondering, "What's the rest of the untold truth?" That was something I would unearth later, and not with a shovel, more like a backhoe tractor.

Chapter Eight
My Wedding Day

Winter, Saturday late morning and no sign of the sun. A layer of white fog slowly dissipated as gentle rain drops collected in puddles. It was six hours before my wedding. I lay stretched out in the bathtub filled with deliciously hot water and surrounded in billowing iridescent lavender-scented bubbles. Steam rose all around me. Wiping the perspiration from my brow with a damp cloth, I realized, in the luxury of that moment, I couldn't stave off the nagging doubts penetrating my thoughts. The minutes ticked closer to my wedding hour, while I pondered recent events.

Two weeks prior, Steve made an appointment with a gynecologist, without my consent. He wanted me to be fit for a diaphragm. I recalled my conversation with the doctor was awkward. She had asked me when my last pap smear was.

My reply was, "This is my first."

She then asked how many sexual encounters I had engaged in.

My answer was, "None."

She looked at me in utter disbelief as though I'd come from another planet. "You're a virgin? You mean to tell me you haven't even had sex with your fiancé?"

I told her my religion doesn't approve of premarital sex.

The doctor called Steve back into the room and briefly explained to him why she did not want to fit me for a diaphragm. She told him it would be uncomfortable and there could possibly be bleeding.

Steve said, "Then I'd like you to put her on birth control pills."

They spoke as though I had no decision to make. I stammered out, "No! I can't. The pill will throw my hormones off balance and it's dangerous. My Mom told me it's a toxic chemical and not to take it."

The doctor told Steve of other alternatives, such as condoms. He said he would only use them temporarily until the pill takes effect. She, looked somewhat puzzled, while she stepped out of the room, and gave the "odd couple" some privacy.

Steve threatened me, that if I became pregnant, I'd find him hanging from the rafters with a noose around his neck. Because I was a naïve seventeen-year-old, I believed he meant it. Now, in my more seasoned years, I realize that was another classic manipulation tactic. So, Steve triumphantly instructed the doctor to put me on the pill.

While enjoying the hot water surrounding me, I pondered his treatment of me four days prior, when we decorated our home.

Liz volunteered to help Steve and I unpack. We had been unpacking for a couple hours, when Liz decided to step out into the cool evening air for a walk. I hummed about the house contentedly, visualizing my new life with Steve. I noticed our new corner table needed a center piece. I cocked my head to the side and wondered what to put there. My light bulb flashed, *Yes, of course!* I stepped out onto the front porch and retrieved my small leafy Boston fern along with its blue saucer and placed it on the table. I stood back and admired my decision.

In the kitchen, I removed newspaper from individually wrapped glasses and cups and placed them into the cupboard. When I returned to the living room, I noticed the Boston fern was gone. *That's weird*, I thought while scanning the living room. It was nowhere in sight. I stepped out onto the porch and there it was back in its original spot. I scooped it up and set it back on the table. A few minutes later, the same thing happened again. *Okay, what's going on here?* I stepped outside and grabbed it once again when Steve barked loudly from behind, "No!" I nearly dropped the fern, I was shocked he used that tone with me.

He barked a second time, "Put the plant back, now!"

I asked in disbelief, "Why can't I have the plant here?"

"Because it will leak on the table."

"But I put a saucer under it to catch the water, see?"

"I want you to put the plant back, now!" He ordered.

A warm prickly flush, swept over me; my chest tightened, and I was unable to breath (I suffered from asthma whenever I was faced with stress.). My legs felt shaky.

After returning the fern, I walked into the second bedroom, unlatched the old rusty antique lock on the casement, and lifted the heavy creaking window as high as it was willing. I hung my head out and inhaled the cool night air. I was feeling strange and beginning to question Steve's actions.

I wondered if maybe I was just feeling a little sensitive. Just a couple of hours before, we had all stopped off at the gas station. Steve and Liz waited in the truck for me, while I ran in to use the bathroom. When I came back outside, I walked up to the truck to get in, when Steve backed out of the driveway and drove away with Liz in the truck with him. They both laughed while pointing at me. They returned five minutes later. When they came back, they were still laughing. However, I didn't find it amusing; in fact, it hurt my feelings. While my head still hung out the window, I continued breathing the air deep into my lungs, hoping it would ease the pressure in my chest.

Steve stepped into the room and asked, "What's wrong with you, Aubri?" My throat tightened, and my eyes burned. He then questioned, "Are you still taking the pill?"

I told him, "Yes,"

"Good, now maybe you should pull yourself together. Liz will be back soon, she'll wonder why you're acting strange."

And now, I soaked nervously in hot sudsy water, feeling a little dizzy from the heat. Carefully repositioning myself so as not to splash water over the edge, I leaned forward like a drooping daisy in need of water and hung my head over the bathtub's edge. My Mom came into the bathroom, took one concerned look at her limp daughter, and asked, "Aubrey, are you okay? You're so pale."

I told her "I think it might be the pill."

"The pill?" she said. "Tell me you're not taking the pill. The side effects are damaging. They'll throw your hormones off balance." She became very angry with Steve for selfishly disregarding my feelings and pleaded with me not to take them. Weak, and nervous of the wedding hour approaching, I appeased my Mom and told her I'd stop taking the pill.

Three o'clock in the afternoon, the tires of my father's unusual-shade-of-violet-blue Mercedes crunched into the gravel driveway of the Kingdom Hall parking lot. My sisters and I stepped out of the car, carrying our dresses and cosmetic bags. We were ushered into the building and temporarily tucked away in a makeshift bridal room.

As we primped in mirrors, the hustle and bustle just outside the door was slowly building with a somewhat hushed excitement. The florist delivered lavender roses and sweet-scented white freesia bouquets. Dad and Luke placed large Boston ferns onto white faux Roman pillars placed on each side of the platform, while Mom gave last minute touch up instructions.

The hour glass had dropped nearly all its sand. Nervously, I sat with my stomach in knots and stared at my reflection in the mirror. *It's too late to cancel; people came from near and far to witness our wedding, Mom wouldn't stand for it, she's basically taken over the wedding as if it's her own.* The red flags were demanding my attention! Sadly, I ignored the words of wisdom. Numerous warnings had been ignored.

My sisters looked beautiful in their long flowing gowns and garlands of delicate baby's breath and baby roses in their hair. Susan wore a deep shade of burgundy as my Maid of Honor. Liz wore light dusty rose and my darling baby sister Anne, my flower girl, wore pink. And, of course my best friend Luke my twelve-year-old brother was my ring bearer. Luke, being my closest friend, should have been my Man of honor, however according to my Mom, wedding protocol takes precedence. My dress was elegant, yet simple. Being a country girl, I was more impressed with the label reading, "Made in New York City." With long-laced sleeves that belled at my wrists, and a beaded bodice that fit snugly to my tiny waist, the material was heavy, enabling it to hang straight down with a semi-long train. My veil was a lovely, white-beaded cap with four feet of lace flowing from it; combs and bobby pins were required to hold it in place. I placed the last of many bobby pins in my cap and gave it a gentle tug for safe measure.

My heart jumped and sped faster while hearing the music and my sisters filed out one by one. Now alone in the room and standing in silent contemplation, I gently pulled the veil over my face— little did I know, metaphorically, I pulled a veil over my life. While attempting to steady my nerves by breathing deeply, my trembling hand reached down and grasped onto the door knob. Slowly, I opened the door: to my painful lessons... My karma... My life.

My father approached me, wearing his brushed silk and cotton blue-gray suit. He gave me his classic blue-eyed wink. Smiling, he said, "You look beautiful, Aubri Rose," and offered me his forearm. Gratefully, I grabbed on. We slowly approached the main room. There were hundreds of people; every seat had been taken, and roughly fifty friends were standing to witness our wedding.

In wedding step elegance, we made our way down the aisle and there, on stage, was Steve, standing in all his glory. He wore his white tuxedo and a nervous, intoxicated grin. Dad handed me over to his future son-in-law, as we listened to a long and tedious sermon.

Then came the part everyone anxiously awaits. We exchanged our vows and placed rings on each other's fingers. The preacher made his announcement, "You may now kiss your bride." The words rang loudly in my ears, reverberating with a sound like a prison door slamming behind me.

I investigated Steve's eyes as he grinned his unnerving smile. He lifted the veil over my head and pulled me firmly into his arms. His breath reeked of whiskey as he kissed me hard and deliberate. My burgundy-colored lipstick (hardly a discreet color) smeared over my cheeks and chin. I heard shocked gasps and some people roared with laughter. My veil began slipping off my head, the pins I'd so carefully applied scraped and pulled at my hair and scalp, while Steve continued kissing me. He finally released me from his controlling grip.

We were instructed to turn around and face the crowd of four-hundred friends and family members. My cheeks were red from embarrassment. One of my hands held my veil in place, while shyly, yet hardly discreetly, I de-smudged my lipstick with my other. We were greeted with loud applause and cheering as a newly married couple.

Chapter Nine
My Cage

We ate, drank, danced, opened gifts, and smiled ten thousand times for our trigger happy friends flashing cameras before us. My cheeks were never as sore as they were that Winter day. We received hugs and kisses from friends I hadn't seen years.

My favorite Uncle Jimmy handed me a chilled glass of Riesling and suggested I take one sip each time I was hugged. "It takes the edge off," he joked. Because I was only seventeen, I was hardly an experienced drinker. Nevertheless, I innocently took the suggested advice. Voices swirled around me like trumpet blasts. Although not drunk (thank God), I decided to do as the expression says and nip that bit of advice in the bud. Had I not, you would have found me plastered face first in our four-tiered wedding cake. Roughly five hours passed and nearly everyone had gone, except for the few remaining on the dance floor enjoying the music, and the last of the wine.

We said our goodbyes and left the reception hall; Steve grabbed my butt and said to me firmly, "You're mine now, Aubri!"

Bed & Breakfast

Around 10:00PM, we arrived at our Bed and Breakfast in beautiful Napa Valley: a place where tourists came from all around the world, visiting wineries and capturing on film gondolas scattered in the vineyards, and laden with the New Year's harvest. Truly an enchanting season, with breathtaking fall colors. Crimson reds, golden hues, copper orange and rustic purple, spread like a colorful blanket over the foothills and vineyard countryside.

Steve and I pulled into the driveway of a lovely Spanish-style Villa tucked away in the outskirts of Saint Helena. We walked along a cobblestone path softly lit with landscape lighting. The path weaved and meandered through beautifully manicured gardens. The cool night air had a sharp bite of winter approaching. I breathed in the intoxicating aroma of wood smoke gently billowing above each chimney, from the roof tops of our Villa. We checked in at the front desk, received our key, and went straight to our honeymoon suite.

We entered our room; my peaceful moment abruptly ended when Steve's demeanor changed. He sternly said, "We need to talk about why you decided to stop taking the pill."

"They weren't agreeing with me, Steve. My hormones were starting to get thrown off. I don't feel comfortable taking them, and besides, my Mom's upset too. She asked me to stop taking them, so I stopped taking them today."

"I want you to go and get the pills."

"I can't, I promised my Mom."

His voice sounded as though he were trying to mask his anger. He spoke slowly as he enunciated each word clearly, *"You will get the pills now!"*

I retrieved my purse, reached for the pink plastic container, and sat down on the edge of the bed. Meanwhile, Steve filled a glass with water and handed it to me. Hovering above me like a vulture, he took the plastic container from my hand, removed one tiny white pill from the foil wrapper and placed it in my hand. Briefly, I analyzed the toxic pill as I rolled it around in my palm. *I thought he loved me. Why is he not respecting me? My feelings don't matter to him.* As I pondered over his lack of concern, he barked out, "TAKE THE PILL, NOW!" Startled by his tone, I quickly popped it into my mouth and swallowed it down fast with water. The pit in my stomach tightened as a warm flush of shock swept over me.

He patted me on the head and spoke like a caring father, "Now you see, that wasn't so bad, was it?" An odd mixture of sensations rose within me. I silently thought, *you see, he does love you. He said he's proud of you*. However, the penetrating chill in my bones could not be shaken.

Satisfied in gaining control, Steve briskly rubbed his hands together and asked with a grin, "Are you going to change into something?" So, off to the bathroom I went and closed the door behind me.

As far back as memory serves, I've had a belief system that clearly ran deep. However, being a strong-willed child and speaking one's inner truth were not acceptable with my parents or my religion. Unfortunately, my freedom of speech was squelched with the end of my Dad's belt or the wooden spoon Mom used frequently. In time, my independence was broken, like that of a wild mustang learning to adjust to a bridle stuck in her mouth and a heavy saddle thrown on her back. Kicking and bucking under the weight of an uncaring rider, and no longer able to withstand the metal spurs digging into her sides, she quickly mastered the art of gulping down her deeply wounded feelings. And now? I shockingly realized my perceived Savior was not a savior. He was a heavy handed uncaring rider. So, my voice was merely a whisper from my past.

My survival coping skills were: never talk back, never question, and my facial expression was smile, smile, and smile more.

While staring at my reflection in the mirror, I leaned over the bathroom sink and splashed cool water on my face. The simple, clean gesture usually calmed me, but not this time. So, on went my "survival smile" and a white silk nightgown. That was the first time I had worn anything slinky to bed; I was used to snugly nighties or comfy pajamas. I glanced one final time at the scared girl staring back at me in the mirror, wearing a fake, nervous smile. Reaching down, I grasped onto the cool metal knob and opened the door...

The following morning, I lay in bed as Steve showered. The entire evening was etched in my mind. I felt numb and in a state of shock, my body sore and aching. My only comfort was the warm rays of the morning sun streaming through the window and the sound of song birds just outside. Determined to stave off the feeling of nausea, I pulled back the blankets to get out of bed. Much to my surprise, there was blood all over the sheets and numerous bloodied condoms strewn on the floor beside the bed. A person might wonder; can a person be raped by a husband or wife? From my personal experience I will say: yes, you can.

Before we checked out of our room, I stripped the soiled sheets off the bed, and rolled them into a ball (not wanting to upset the maid.). I picked the condoms up off the floor and placed them in the waste basket. Steve asked, "What are you doing?" I didn't feel an explanation was needed as I continued picking them up. Much to my astonishment, he told me to "Leave them on the floor. It's the maid's job. Besides, I'm proud of it. She'll know you're a virgin and think 'that lucky girl—she's married to an animal.'"

Later that day, we drove to San Francisco; our destination the following morning: Hawaii. We checked into our motel room near the airport at 6:00PM. Steve suggested we take a shower together. I thought to myself, *Oh, my goodness, I'm too embarrassed*. I felt vulnerable and shy; I was far too bashful to strip down and shower with him. He went to the bathroom and turned on the water, when he returned he looked surprised I wasn't getting ready to shower. He reprimanded me, "Come on, stop being ridiculous and take off your clothes." I shrugged my shoulders in utter embarrassment. He was obviously not happy, his hidden flames could no longer hide beneath his smoldering surface, he demanded, "Get out of your clothes and get in the shower!" His eruption startled me, and I started to cry.

He left the motel room in a frustrated rage. He returned and hour later holding a brown paper bag, containing whiskey and pornographic magazines. He removed his clothes, got into bed and told me to do the same. He forced me to drink the whiskey. I swallowed hard as the fiery liquid burned its way down my throat. He insisted I take a couple more swallows and then look at porn with him. I was in shock! I had never seen pornography before, in fact it was against our religion, *so why would Steve be forcing me?* I wondered. He pointed to one specific picture and told me, "This is what I want you to do." He grabbed my head with both his hands and forced me to give him what he desired. I felt like I was in a nightmare that I couldn't wake up from. He disgusted and repulsed me. I couldn't breathe and gaged; then the tears came. Steve no longer could achieve arousal, so he did what abusers do and masterfully turned the blame onto me. "Oh, just forget it," he yelled, "You don't know what you're doing." He rolled over and went to sleep. Sadly, being an abused young woman, I took on the shame and the guilt as though I had done something wrong; so essentially, I was punishing myself as well.

The following afternoon, we arrived in beautiful Maui. We stepped off the plane, welcomed with tropical music and beautiful Island people. They greeted us with alohas and lovely, sweet-scented floral leis. I became mesmerized by the lush beauty all around us. Blossoming fragrant plants and orchids grew abundantly, hundreds of tall, sleek palm trees stood gracefully lining the beaches, contrasting with the vibrant blue of the Pacific Ocean. The sunsets looked as though God painted magnificent watercolor masterpieces in the sky.

A week had passed; things progressively got worse. One afternoon, we visited a tourist area. We strolled up a well-traveled path, which eventually lead to a waterfall. We approached an old rustic bridge and began walking across it; I greeted people in passing along the way. At one point, Steve stopped, while I continued walking. He hollered out to me, "Hey, come back here." I noticed people instinctively stopped and looked at him. I turned and walked back to him. Steve instantly reached out and pulled my bright green tube top down to my waist, revealing my bare breasts. He then pointed at me and laughed repeatedly. I stood mortified in broad daylight with nowhere to hide while I quickly pulled my top up.

Hot & Cold

Steve had bought a book to read while on vacation. His nose was stuck in it quite a bit of the time. One morning, I decided to hide it from him. While he searched for his book, he asked me if I had seen it anywhere. My playful response was, "Why don't we play hot and cold and you can try to find it?" My intention was to lighten the mood and to be silly!

He searched for a few minutes; each time he heard cold, colder and then freezing, he got agitated. It was no longer a game for him. He grabbed hold of me and began tickling me. It wasn't a tickle I was accustomed to; he pressed his fingertips aggressively into my ribs and "tickled." He continued without letting up until I was unable to breathe. His tight grip made it impossible for me to break away. I wanted to scream out, "Let me go!" but I had no air left in my lungs. A wave of panic washed over me as he continued his aggressive tickling. *"Oh, my God, I can't breathe!"* I panicked. When he finally released me, I fell to the floor gasping. Then, in an aggressive voice, he said, "Now, are you going to tell me where my book is?"

Before I had a chance to think about what I was going to say, I blurted out, "I HATE YOU!" Oops! It was too late to retract the words. They hung briefly in the air before hitting the carpet with a shocking explosion. The color drained from my face, as I wondered, *"Will he hurt me?"* I was shocked I said that to Steve! The last time I said those words were to Liz on that fateful Summer evening.

Quickly, I ran to the book's hiding place and returned his leather-bound pages. His expression was of shock. He left the room fuming with anger and took his book with him. For the next few days, he refused to talk to me. Once again, the typical co-dependent as well as the people pleaser in me thought nothing of the fact that he purposely tickled me to the point of nearly passing out. My mental dialogue played over and over. *"He didn't realize he was hurting me. He was only playing. It's all my fault. I never should have hidden his book and I never should have said "I hate you". He has every right not to talk to me."*

One late afternoon, Steve's parents called our motel room to speak with of us. I sat anxiously on the edge of the bed waiting my turn to say hi. His conversation began to wind down, I knew it was only a matter of seconds before I would have the opportunity to talk with them. Steve looked at me and grinned a creepy grin. What I heard him say next startled me awake! "Oh, you wanna talk to Aubrianna? Well, you can't she isn't here. She went out for a walk."

There was a slight pause. He then said, "Yeah okay, I'll tell her you said hi."

Perplexed and amazed, drawing my brows together and silently questioned, *did he really just say that? Why would he lie to them?* I left the motel room while he still spoke to his parents. I inhaled the warm salty air while gazing out over the waters. I sat with my legs drawn up under me, my chin supported by my knees, while wiggling my toes in the warm soothing sand. The ocean water was calm and the sky a radiant shade of burnt orange and brilliant aqua blue. The sun began its mesmerizing descent and sunk silently into the ocean. My heart felt heavy with a curious melancholy feeling as I contemplated what had just transpired.

Later that evening, I apprehensively asked, "Steve, why did you say that to your parents?" "Why did I say what?" He acted flippantly as though he had no idea what I was talking about.

"You told them I was outside when they asked to speak with me."

"Yeah, so what?" His casual reply disturbed me.

Suddenly everything became crystal clear; I had married a man with serious issues. Myself as well for that matter. The warm tropical beauty of the island wasn't enough to ease the cool chill creeping into my bones.

Free Me From My Cage

Bird in the Cage

Two long weeks had passed; our "Honeymoon" was over. The plane landed in cold and foggy San Francisco. Steve's parents were waiting for us in the Baggage Claim area. We briefly embraced (his parents were not the warm and fuzzy hugging type). We retrieved our luggage and were soon in his parents' car. Our next stop was home to see my family for a welcome back dinner.

We pulled into the driveway; the car headlights penetrated the fog as we slowly weaved our way up the gravel driveway and parked beside the row of Cedar trees. The porch light glowed in the evening dampness like a beacon of hope. A lump formed in my throat as I saw my family coming to the front door, waiting for me in excited anticipation.

Ezra, our black German shepherd, approached the car. His deep threatening growl and sharp fangs were enough to keep any stranger from getting out of their vehicle. He relaxed his furrowed hair and put away his fangs, when he saw me get out of the car. The cool, damp air and the scent of our pine trees was welcoming. We walked up the path to the front entrance and to my family's open arms.

Now inside, we stood around the fireplace warming our cold backsides. Mom, the perfect hostess, offered hot toddies to Steve and my new in-laws. When Dad saw my neck covered in hickies, and I do mean covered in hickies!, he was not happy, I heard him say under his breath, "Maybe we need to get Steve a pacifier."

Eventually, I broke away from the group to join my sisters in Susan's room. Their faces were glowing with excitement, anxious to find out every detail of the honeymoon. They gasped when they saw my neck and wanted to know all about the sex. However, much to their surprise, they had a paranoid sister, nervously peering over her shoulder, and wanting to make sure the door was closed. Susan, the intuitive mother, drew her brows together, "Aubri, what's wrong?" she asked lovingly.

The tears came; I couldn't control them, and soon I was gagging through sobs! Mom stepped into the room and her expression instantly changed when she saw me. I tried whispering through the growing lump in my throat. "Mom", "I shouldn't have married him. He's not who I thought he was. I don't want to go home with him, he's abusive, he scares me!" I pleaded.

Moms reply was, "Aubri, you're just getting to know each other, and you know how Jehovah feels about a divorcing." I looked at her through tear-filled eyes. Feeling as though I were in court, with the final decision hanging on the jury. I stood before the judge awaiting the verdict... The gavel dropped! She announced her decision. It echoed loudly in my ears! *YOU ARE MARRIED TO THIS MAN FOR THE REST OF YOUR LIFE, YOUR LIFE, YOUR LIFE, YOUR LIFE!*

And, so it was... The white bird hung her head low and drew her clipped wings closely to her side. She stepped into the cold, dark metal cage. The heavy door heaved shut and locked with a cruel and brutal finality!

Chapter Ten

Our New Home

Our wedding was over. And, I was learning to adapt to marriage and life in Saint Helena. Three weeks prior to our wedding, we had found an affordable rental home, and only a three-block walk into town. A charming 1940's white stucco home which just so happened to need a lot of care. The overgrown bottle brush and holly bushes blocked sunlight from the living and dining room windows. The side yard had two enormous Meyer lemon trees in need of a serious pruning makeover, and the over-grown lawn was filled with clumps of dandelions and dry patches from irregular watering. The back yard was dry and barren, except for the old weathered clothes line, which technically still made it barren.

Inside was somewhat dreary with two small bedrooms and one tiny bathroom with barely enough room to turn around in. The spacious kitchen was brightly lit with outdoor light streaming in through the windows. The entire home was heated with an outdated gas floor heater. When turned on, it made a rather disconcerting igniting sound, as if it might blow up. It smelled gassy, as though it leaked fuel. Despite all our home's faults, I visualized it transformed into my little honeymoon cottage.

We later discovered that the cold damp home came complete with an Entity. It had been a relief for me to leave behind the mean spirit in the Healdsburg home, but then to discover another spirit was discouraging to say the least. Although it never materialized— *thank you!* —it's main hang out was in the kitchen. Usually, every evening between the hours of 9:00 and 11:00, it would create a loud sound, as though a ball was being bounced on the kitchen floor. The first few times we heard it, we went to the kitchen to investigate the strange sound and were perplexed to find nothing each time! Not knowing of the tenant that came with the house, we decided to make it our future "honeymoon pad" at a low rental cost of $325 a month.

Some friends of Steve's were preparing for a garage sale. They'd asked if we'd like to view the furniture before the stampeding public arrived? So off we went on a treasure hunt. I loved yard sales, they sent adrenaline straight to my veins, like a thoroughbred galloping straight to the finish line. I couldn't get out of a vehicle fast enough; for surely someone might find the "valuable junk" before me.

When we arrived in Steve's red 57 Chevy truck, I felt that familiar rush. An antique sofa, chair, and ottoman combination caught my attention, although the unusual shade of olive green would take getting used to. I was thrilled with the solid maple claw foot legs and diamond tucked upholstery. I asked for Steve's permission, he gave me the "green light" nod of approval. We also found a coffee table and a matching end table. They weren't much to be desired since the fake wood had deep scratches. However, with the help of a couple doilies or plants, *voilà*, the problem would be solved. I was delighted with our new-found treasures, all for the bargain price of $25.

Steve's Controlling Behavior

I was married and physically living in our house. Only thing was that it didn't feel like mine, anything I did had to have Steve's approval at all times. The effects of loneliness were settling in—no brothers, sisters, nieces, or nephews. I had grown accustomed to the Grand Central Station hustle and bustle of friends dropping in unexpectedly.

Because Steve was an only child, he didn't understand; his parents were more the reclusive sort. Unfortunately, he wouldn't allow me to drive either, which only added to my feelings of being shut off from the outside world.

Strangely, he taught me how to drive when we dated. What I didn't know then was, he had no intention of letting me drive once we were married. He told me, "You can walk. You don't need to drive anywhere."

For myself, I was suffering from child hood traumas, as well as being a classic people pleaser, a co-dependent, and now let's just throw into the mix, a physically and verbally abused teen ager. When we're unaware of how to protect ourselves from cruel malicious comments and behavior, then our emotional disturbances will only worsen. Mental abuse, begins by eroding us from the inside out. Like a parasitical disease, sucking away our life force. Robbing us of self-esteem, taking away our joy for life, Shockingly, it becomes an insidious part of who we think we are, which essentially is who we become.

Sadly, I was giving Steve silent permission to brain wash me. I believed in the lies he told me.

Eating Disorder

Anxiety, depression, awkwardness, and walking on eggshells around Steve's ever shifting personality had me plummet deeper into loneliness. Love and affection was my main priority; however, it was nothing I would get from Steve. So, I turned to food as my "savior". My weight fluctuated by ten pounds. Days would go by when I ate nothing, and other days I'd eat whatever junk food was available. I was humiliated when I didn't have any self-control. Sometimes, I'd eat an entire bag of chips, or an entire bag of cookies. At times, Steve would reach into the cupboard for a snack and find nothing.

"Where are the chips or the cookies?" he'd inquire.

I was mortified when I had to explain to him the first time, "I ate them; I'm so sorry, we can get more."

He looked me up and down with disgust and spewed belittling remarks, "God, what a pig! Your disgusting!"

Depression began staking claim! I found myself sleeping most the day; I felt as though I was slipping into a hazy slow motion world, far from outside contact, outside stimulation. After several months of spiraling deeper, I realized it would take strength for me to be disciplined, otherwise I'd fall completely into depression. So, I came up with a "stay-busy outdoors" approach. After Steve's breakfast, I jogged to a nearby junior high school before it opened and played solo tennis against the back wall. I then jogged home and got dressed for preaching work, then waited for a congregation member to pick me up and take me to Calistoga twelve miles away.

Steve, as I mentioned earlier, wouldn't let me drive, nor would he give me any allowance, which was cause for embarrassment, because I couldn't contribute gas money. And equally embarrassing when we took coffee and donut breaks; Jehovah's Witnesses are known for never missing out on coffee and donut breaks! All the Brothers and Sisters sipped on coffee and ate scrumptious goodies, while I sat and watched. To add more embarrassment fuel to the fire, my reputation was poor penniless Aubri, which had friends asking probing questions, such as: "Why doesn't Steve give you an allowance?" "Why doesn't he let you drive?" "Do you want to borrow some money?"

No Time

One Summer morning, I had a job interview; I would be cleaning a wealthy woman's home once a week. She lived in a gorgeous upscale neighborhood of Saint Helena. It also just so happened she lived about 20 minutes away. On the day of my interview, I was running late and knew I didn't have time to ride my bike. Concerned I wouldn't get the job, I decided to grab the truck keys. Minutes later, I was barreling down Pope Street going thirty-five in a twenty-five-mile zone, when I noticed a police car with lights flashing. Nervously, I kept driving, only because I was unsure of just what it was I was supposed to do, until I heard a loud speaker: "Pull your vehicle over now!" I jumped and nervously did as instructed and pulled into a dirt ditch beside an orchard.

The towering male figure asked me for my license.

I told him, "I don't have it."

He stated firmly, "Do you realize that's against the law and I could write you up for driving without your license?"

I innocently said, "No officer, that's not what I mean."

"Well, what do yah mean?" he brusquely inquired. "I don't have a license!"

His expression was of disbelief, "You mean to tell me you don't have a driver's license?"

I sheepishly explained to him my husband doesn't allow me to drive, and that I was late for a job interview up the road a few miles, and that's why I drove.

His surprising reply was, "Honey, tell yah what, you go ahead and drive to your interview and when you're done, you drive straight home. If I ever see you driving again, you'd better have a license!" "Okay," I said with relief.

He wished me luck on my job interview as I drove away.

In case you're curious whether I got the job—I did. And once a week I left my house a half hour earlier on my bike. The great thing about having that job was that even though I gave Steve nearly my entire paycheck, I got to keep a small amount, which I used for contributing to gas money, and for those delicious coffee and donut breaks!

Perfectionist

One form of Steve's punishment was his refusal to talk with me. I called it the silent treatment. His "anger barometer" determined how long he'd shut me out.

If there were an Oscar in the best co-dependent category, I'd have won! There could be no worse punishment than Steve not speaking to me. I needed his approval at all costs! Him not speaking to me was devastating. As the expression says, I bent over backwards. My goodness! I did more than that, I bent over backwards and Snapped!

Sadly, I allowed myself to be subjected to an onslaught of critical abuse. My naturally endowed breasts were not shaped to his liking and my nipples were not the right color. "Why do you have to wear your hair that way? I like your hair dark; do you have to gulp your water so loudly?" My knees and elbows are double jointed, so he constantly told me, "Gross, that's disgusting, stand with your legs forward so I don't have to see your knees bend back." Or, "Your skin's too white, why couldn't you have darker skin?" Etc... Etc... Etc...

Being raised by a mother with high expectations, I perceived perfection as the only way to please my mother, and now I felt it was the only way to please Steve. Henceforth, I aimed high, I aimed for the impossible.

So... In my attempts of pleasing him, I baked in the sun to darken my fair skin and became a chameleon by coloring my honey colored hair various shades of brown, black, red, mahogany, or bombshell blonde. I darkened my nipples with brown eye shadow and trained myself not to relax my knees and elbows. And any time he was around me while I was drinking, I would take the tiniest sip and nervously swallow with no sound. Desperately, I wanted to please him, but sadly, he was never satisfied, only annoyed. I found myself walking in a field of land mines, unable to spot the triggers buried beneath his surface.

Regardless of his cruel treatment, I continued my persistent neediness. One afternoon, about an hour before Steve would be home, I riffled through my closet looking for just the right dress to wear. I found exactly what I wanted—my powder blue, full-length summer dress. It had gathered short sleeves, a low scooped neckline, and a blue silk ribbon tied in a bow centered just under my sternum for enhancing my bust line. (A dress I wasn't allowed to wear outside of the house.) I applied my makeup and sprayed his favorite Babe cologne behind my ears, on each wrist and on my cleavage. Then, I brushed and styled my hair. The reflection was that of a beautiful young woman, though I never knew it.

I set the dining room table hours in advance, complete with white cloth napkins rolled neatly and held in place with napkin rings, plates, salad bowls, silverware, and salt and pepper grinders. The centerpiece held an elegant sterling silver candelabra displaying three slender white candles. I'd prepared one of Steve's favorites: steak, baked potatoes, biscuits, and salad.

Anxiously, I awaited Steve's return while watching the monotonous movement of the clock lethargically ticking one minute at a time. Steve pulled into the driveway and my heart sped up. I ran to the front door like a loyal puppy wagging her tail, greeting him with a big smile. Before entering the house, he looked over his shoulder to make sure no males in our neighborhood might have seen me.

He asked me, "What's for dinner?"

Teasingly, I replied, "I can't tell you. It's a surprise."

He left the room to take a shower before dinner. While Steve was cleaning up, I finished setting the table and lit the candles. I scrutinized the table making sure I hadn't overlooked any details; I wanted everything to be perfect. Somehow, Steve was always able to find something wrong.

We sat down. "Ah, my favorite, steak and potatoes," he smiled. I watched him with anticipation as he briefly scanned the table. *So far, so good* I nervously thought. Steve reached beside his plate for his knife and pulled up a butter knife. He drew his eyebrows together and was silent for a moment.

He then looked at me and started laughing as he shook his head and smirked, "Are you stupid?"

My bright smile faded as I nervously replied, "I don't understand, what do you mean?"

"Who cuts their steak with a butter knife? Only an idiot would!"

I desperately fought back my tears and kindly replied, "Oh ... I'm so sorry. Here let me get you a steak knife."

"No, that's okay, I'll get it myself." He gruffly said, as he left the table and walked to the kitchen.

Verbal Abuse

There are different levels of verbal abuse. Some verbal abuse is done in a sneaky, under-handed way. The abuser will turn a situation around on the victim, making it appear as if it's his or her fault. That's phycological abuse, which causes a person to question their sanity, and therefore excusing the abuser's behavior: In fact, verbal abuse is far more dangerous than physical abuse. By no means am I underestimating physical abuse. It's a horrible, life threatening, and demoralizing experience to be physically harmed, especially from someone claiming to love you. The terrifying effect of verbal abuse is what it does to our mind. The innocent victim is essentially having his or her brain raped!

Cruel Games

Steve was notorious for playing games, one of which was, deliberately tripping me. He only did it now and then, so he could catch me off guard. When I entered a room and walked past him, he would stick his foot out to trip me, and I'd fall to the floor. He'd then point at me, laughing and nodding his head as though I were an idiot, "When are you gonna get it? Most people would have figured it out, by now."

A gruesome game he enjoyed, which absolutely terrified me. (Ironically, the game he made up was before any of the chain *Saw* movies came out.) He pretended to hold a chainsaw above his head. He pulled the starter rope; the engine sputtered (he made the sputtering noise and the sound effects) He pulled it again, building the chilling suspense; it continued to sputter. He pulled harder! Then suddenly, the motor ignited with a daunting scream! He chased after me, slashing at my arms and legs. He slowed down the engine noise while pretending to cut through my bones. As I said, it terrified me, however to him, it was just a game.

Another obsession of Steve's was to watch violent movies. He wanted his "buddy" (that would be me) to watch them with him. Now, I had always appreciated a good Alfred Hitchcock thriller; however, I drew the line with violent films. They abhorred me and frightened me for weeks afterwards. I couldn't stomach seeing people hacked up while blood spewed out of every orifice, nor seeing people haunted by evil poltergeists. If I freaked out, his usual reply was, "Oh, come on, loosen up. Why do you have to be so uptight?" So, what did I do? I compromised my values and watched one shocking bloody film after another.

Free Me From My Cage

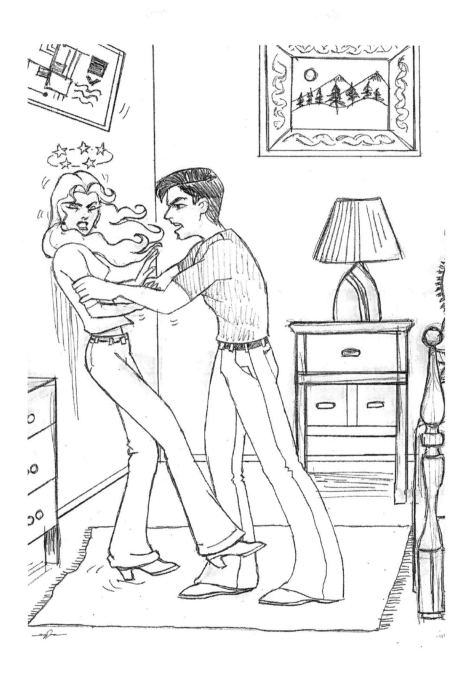

Seeing Stars

I became masterful at disguising my bruises, makeup and turtlenecks did the trick. In time, Steve became wiser. He no longer left bruises on my neck or face; he would hit my head against walls instead. I remember the first time I saw stars before passing out. I didn't know seeing stars was real; I thought it was only something you saw in cartoons.

One morning, Steve and I awoke to the alarm sounding off much earlier than normal. We were going to a religious convention in San Francisco for the day. I felt depressed and exhausted, and didn't want to be with friends asking the newly-wed couple the usual question, "How's married life, guys?" Far too often, I'd get emotional and cry when friends hugged me; surprised, they'd look at Steve. I feared my causing a scene would create more problems behind closed doors. So, I usually spoke quickly, "Oh, I'm just crying because I haven't seen you in a long time, I'm so happy to see you." On this particular morning, I couldn't face getting out of bed and plastering on a large fake smile.

Steve got out of bed and took a shower. Thirty minutes later he came back into our room, dressed in his three-piece white suit and perfectly straight yellow tie. "What, are you still doing in bed? Get up!" he barked.

"I can't go, I'm too tired." I moaned.

"You're going, so get up, now!"

I crawled out of bed and went to the closet in search of a dress and heels. I felt emotionally overwhelmed and wanted to hide under the covers from Steve and the world. "I can't do this," I said, as I crawled back into bed and pulled the blankets up over me.

Steve entered the room and yanked back the covers. He grabbed me by the arm and pulled me limply to the floor. "Get up, you lazy bitch," he demanded.

"I can't, I just can't. Steve, I'm too tired," I replied through tears of exhaustion. How does a person tell an abusive man she's depressed and doesn't want to face her friends probing questions?

He kicked at me, shoving me hard with his foot and yelling abusively, "You're so stubborn and lazy." I lay there on the floor allowing him to kick at me as though I were a defenseless, wounded animal (and, in a sense, I was). He eventually gave up. He straightened his posture, adjusted his tie and walked out the front door in his flawless white suit and reputation.

Sunday morning, the congregation was seated and listening to a Bible discourse on Moses coming down off the mountain. Anyone observing Steve and myself might have thought, *"Ahhh, they're so beautiful together. What a sweet couple. Look, he's whispering in her ear. I'll bet he's telling her how much he loves her.* Little do they know, Steve leans over and whispered, "My god, your breath stinks. What have you been doing, eating dog shit?" Steve was always whispering cruel remarks during Bible discourses and I continued choking down my feelings.

Another time, the lights were off as we all watched a slide show on missionaries in Africa. Steve slowly and discreetly slipped his hand up under my skirt and started fondling me. Afraid he'd be angry if I shoved his hand away, I sat nervously scanning the crowd, terrified someone might see.

In our congregation, we were encouraged to mingle before and after the service. However, when Steve was ready to go, I learned from experience not to keep him waiting. So, I needed to keep a hawk eye on his whereabouts. When I'd see him nearing the exit, I'd follow quickly on his heels. One Sunday afternoon, I saw Steve heading in the direction of the back door, so I knew I needed to head that way. As, I began my route to the exit door, I saw "The Chatter Box" coming my way. She was an elderly woman in her eighties known particularly for her long-winded stories. On this particular day, I tried avoiding her penetrating gaze—too late, she snagged me! I was caught with no immediate way out! I panicked, when I saw Steve head out the door.

After a few minutes of talking with the longwinded "Chatter box" I got extremely nervous, because I couldn't disconnect. Her hearing aid buzzed a high-pitched squeal and her dentures rattled in her mouth while she chatted of high blood pressure, arthritis, and constipation troubles. "Oh, my goodness, that's terrible," I replied while anxious thoughts raced through my head. Roughly ten minutes had passed when I victoriously broke free! I frantically made my way to the back door as brothers and sisters smiled and asked me how I was doing. I walked past each potential road block with my plastered-on smile and usual reply, "I'm doing great, thank you!" I quickly walked out the back door, made my way to the truck and apologized to Steve for being late.

He didn't speak as we slowly drove away from the parking area. A friend crossing the street in front of us waved goodbye, but he ignored the friendly gesture. Sweetly, I said, "Steve? Katherine waved to us. We should wave to her, so she doesn't get her feelings hurt." Next thing I knew, he back handed me, and split open my lower lip. I clasped my hand over my mouth as drops of blood trickled down my chin. He yelled at me to stop crying, so I tried silencing my whimpers through muffled gags.

He took his hand off the steering wheel, grabbed me by my blouse and shook me violently. My beaded white blouse ripped off my shoulder as he yelled again telling me to shut up! I panicked and began trembling violently. I cried hysterically while tears flowed down my cheeks, diluting the blood oozing from my lip.

He drove roughly two miles down the road and pulled the truck over. He lowered his voice, attempting to stay composed, and apologized for hurting me and ruining my blouse. "You just shouldn't tell me who I should wave to, that's all." He "tenderly" kissed my cheek and began sexually fondling me. I felt a sick feeling in my stomach as though I'd vomit. I wanted to relieve my pent-up frustrations by screaming with such severity my throat would bleed. He then told me to put my sweater on to hide my torn blouse. "My parents are expecting us for lunch. Is there any way you can fix your lip with makeup? And if anyone asks you about it, just tell them you bumped into something," he instructed.

One December evening, it was nearly 10:00PM when Steve and I left the Kingdom Hall and into the icy cold outdoors. I gathered my coat collar tightly around my neck and walked cautiously in my heels across the street to our truck. We were soon on Hwy 29 headed homeward bound to Saint Helena. I quickly rolled down my window to spit out my gum. Steve barked, "Roll your window up! It's cold in here."

"I am, please give me a chance to spit my gum out." He yelled at me for talking back to him.

"I'm trying to roll the window up. Please just give me a chance." One thing you never do with Steve is reason with him.

His face darkened red with rage; he drove with one hand while gesturing wildly with the other. The veins in his neck and temples were strained and popping out as he screamed maliciously. An escalating panic took over my body. I felt frantic, trapped, and terrified he would hit me! I couldn't endure the mental torture any longer. I clasped my hands tightly over my ears to ward off his cruel, penetrating words. I screamed out, "Oh, my god! Oh, my god! Oh, my god! I'm going to go crazy! I got to get out of here." I literally felt, like I could kick and claw my way out of his truck.

When Steve heard my frenzied pleas, he brought the truck to a screeching halt. He screamed inches from my face! "Okay, you wanna get out of here?" Reaching over me, he unlocked the door and shoved it wide open. I hadn't a chance to comprehend what he was doing. He kicked me and with one angry shove pushed me out of the truck. I tumbled hard onto the cold ground, as he barreled quickly down Hwy 29.

I desperately wanted to scream out my anger and cry at the same time. Instead, I lay in dark frozen silence. Roughly twenty minutes had passed and I was freezing, I wondered how I'd get home. It's a twelve mile walk in the dark, and having no other choices, I started walking. I had only been walking ten minutes when I heard a familiar vehicle headed my way. I knew that sound well enough to know it was Steve. I panicked and jumped into a ditch lying flat on my belly in horror that he might find me. I peered through the tall weeds. He was just ahead of me, driving slowly like a hungry predator. Even the truck looked menacing! The engine idled an ominous growl, the grey exhaust fumes were glowing a muted shade of red from the lit tail lights.

I held my breath! My heart thumped! A part of me wanted him to find me so I could get out of the cold. Another part of me was too angry with his abusive ways and would rather stay out all night than go home with him. However, the bitter cold won the mental feud. I brushed away my fear, swallowed my pride, and crawled out of the weeds. The truck came to a stop, I opened the door, and hoisted my stiff cold body back into the warm truck. Much to my surprise, Steve's anger had subsided. I stared out the window and didn't speak nor make one movement, otherwise I might unknowingly set him off in another rage!

Living a Lie

A shocking, and brutal reality was, I had no escape. The thought of suffocating in darkened silence, was more than I could bare. What was left of my spirit, was that of a slight flickering flame of a candle, soon to be snuffed out. I share with you fragments of my life, black and white etchings of memories gone by. Gradually, I began fading into a state of non-existence. My essence was bombarded consistently, with unyielding and harsh cruelty. With no self-esteem, and confidence completely stripped away, I spoke to no one of my ugly dark secret, as it spread like black ink, seeping seductively, into every crevice of my mind.

GOD HATES A DIVORCING! GOD HATES A DIVORCING! The elders zealously and repetitively preached their sermon. Like a sledgehammer, they pounded their scriptures of judgment into my skull! Until I believed that the only way out of my situation was if Steve died or I committed adultery, and if I were to commit adultery, that would also mean, according to my religious belief, that I would be destroyed at Armageddon.

So, I was trapped in my cage with no way out, riddled with anxiety, depression, shame, and psychologically raped! The suffocating reality gripped me for many, many years to follow.

What I found most challenging was living a lie. I was afraid to tell anyone and pretended that everything was great. My family, close friends, and Kingdom Hall members didn't know that Steve was physically and emotionally violating me. My suffering went unnoticed and my silent cries for help went unheard. I continued stuffing my feelings deeper and deeper into my stomach, and my neck felt a constant choking sensation from lack of self-expression.

Winter set in, my cage closed in on me. I rarely left the house and wore the same clothes for several days before laundering them. I didn't give much thought to personal hygiene and my hair was dull and dirty from lack of washing. My home took on my appearance. I sat and watched my favorites on television all day, usually *Little House on the Prairie*, *The Walton's,* and *I Love Lucy*. I wasn't allowed to watch soap operas; my patriarchal husband and religion wouldn't allow us to watch them.

A Ray of Hope

To keep fuel costs down in the cold winter months, I froze in the house during the day. I wore jackets and gloves. I would only turn the heater on about an hour before Steve got home. The interior walls were white stucco and dripped with condensation. Mildew grew out of the dampness, and tiny, nearly microscopic white bugs crawled everywhere. I'm not sure where the bugs came from, but they lasted the entire winter. It brought back my creepy childhood memories of chicken lice. The disturbing feeling was around me every day. Now and then, when I felt motivated, I'd bleach down the walls only to watch the green slowly creep back, as well as the white bugs.

One day, my mother unexpectedly came to visit me with a close friend, Rena, who was one of my favorites. She was a genuinely beautiful woman with an exuberant personality. One late morning around 11:30, I crawled out of bed to see who had knocked at my door. Usually, I didn't answer, but on this day, I did. I opened the door; my appearance took them by surprise. They stepped inside, scoped out their surroundings, and looked shocked! I wished they had let me know of their plans ahead of time, so I could have plowed through the mess in the kitchen. Mom said, while rubbing her hands together, "Honey, it must be forty degrees in here, I can see my breath. Aubri you'll get pneumonia. Why don't you have the heater on?" She noticed the walls and tried disguising her disgust, "Sweetheart, your walls are moldy." I didn't dare tell her about the millions of microscopic white bugs, otherwise she would have really freaked out!

Eventually, they made their way to the kitchen and were met with another frightening sight: dirty dishes with caked-on food covered all the counter space. Mom cheerfully said, "Aubri lets turn on the heater. Why don't you get cleaned up, take a shower and wash your hair? Then, we'll go to our favorite restaurant, St. Georges."

So, while I showered, they scoured! That delightful and unexpected day touched me with a ray of warmth, until it was time for Mom and Rena to leave. I watched sadly from my cage as they drove away.

Chapter Eleven

Employment

Steve's work slowed down considerably during a long rainy winter. I saw a side of him I didn't know existed as he retreated and became depressed. Because I hadn't seen that side of him before, it frightened me. Our income was dwindling, so he asked me to look for employment. So, at eighteen years old, I began working at my first legitimate job at Buchanan's Stationery Store on Main Street in Saint Helena.

I left the house fifteen minutes early and walked to work in the pouring rain with my large umbrella. I absolutely loved working there, it was so stimulating. It smelled deliciously of spicy cinnamon and sweet lavender from candles and potpourri in the gift shop portion.

The owners, Guli and her husband Bill, looked to be in their seventies, salt of the earth kind of people. My wide-eyed innocence was fascinated by Guli, no doubt a worldly woman and an artist. Her oil paintings of exotic Island women hung on the walls. She had traveled to many distant areas of the world, gathering unique trinkets to sell in her shop. Her husband Bill had a cigarette hanging non-stop from the corner of his mouth, whether lit or not. He taught me to shelve things properly. "Anytime you place new items on the shelf, you always place them behind the existing ones. Do you know why?" he'd gruffly ask without allowing a response, as if he'd preached his sermon to ten thousand teenagers.

Guli instructed another employee named "Helga" to teach me the ground rules. Helga was tall and slender and about ten years older than me. Helga usually wore the same clothing every day, wrangler jeans and a western shirt. She had long straight blonde hair, and her face was plain and unfriendly. It didn't take me long to discover her cruel and slightly sadistic side.

Now for me, math was a subject I had difficulty wrapping my brain around. The store didn't have a cash register, which meant I moved with the speed of a turtle. Observing my weakness, Helga zeroed in on the man with "one thousand items," and deliberately had me help him. She loomed over me like a vulture and smiled like a mean nasty cat while I added numbers agonizingly slow.

Meanwhile, the line grew. While beads of sweat formed above my brow, my mind nervously raced, *oh my god, everyone's staring at me. They must think I'm stupid*. I fought back the tears and impulse to run while I continued to add. Helga barked out with pleasure, "Hurry up, can't you go any faster? Don't you know your math?" Deliberately she pushed me hard out of her way, I stumbled into the file cabinet.

She grumbled, "Here, just let me do it." Helga held her head high while adding the numbers with ease. I was fired after only two weeks on the job. Guli kindly said, "Aubrianna, you're a sweet girl, a hard worker, and honest too. However, Helga has informed me we should consider hiring someone with more experience, so I'm going to have to let you go." I walked home from work with shoulders slumped low and afraid to share the news to Steve.

I soon was hired as a store clerk for Montgomery Wards. Dotty, the owner and manager, was such a bright, happy person; heaven sends us gifts in packages, we don't always understand at the time. And little did I know, Dotty would become an antidote for my low self-esteem.

I'll never forget my first day. She had me on the telephone calling customers and letting them know their orders had arrived. I had made roughly twenty successful calls and dialed the next number on the list, while I waited for someone to answer. A friendly woman's voice answered the phone, "Good morning, Montgomery Wards." I panicked and dropped the phone into the receiver! *"Oh, my goodness, how did I dial the store?"* I panicked. Dotty was standing just a few feet away from me, she sighed and said, "Umm, they hung up on me." Mystified, I waited a few minutes and dialed the number again and Dotty answered with the same greeting, "Good afternoon, Montgomery Wards." My cheeks flushed warm with embarrassment. Confused, I slammed the phone down a second time. I thought about it nervously, *"What do I do? I'll get fired for sure or pushed and yelled at."* I decided to explain my dilemma.

Dotty's pretty face didn't get mean and ugly as I had feared, and she didn't fire me. Instead, she giggled, "Oh, so that explains the hang-ups." It turned out her son had placed an order and put the store number on the order form. She explained my worries away and I still had my job! I loved working alongside Dotty. Her enthusiastic personality was so healing for me. I worked for Dotty for one year, until Steve decided he no longer wanted me working and told me I needed to quit.

A year later, he asked me to look for work again. I was hired as a receptionist at a well-known pharmacy and grocery store (the name shall remain anonymous). We had nearly everything our customers needed, and we had the most amazing sales. It seemed like everyone came to town on those days. Two girls worked the cash registers (one of those girls was me) and another girl on each side of us bagged. Because we had cash registers, I had the speed of a jack rabbit.

I remember the day we had our annual sidewalk sale, those days were always insanely busy, and I loved it! We worked at a frenzied pace to keep up with the steady line of people, when guess who should enter the front doors, with her usual intense expression? Helga! I froze! And my heart jumped into my throat! I had not seen her since I'd been fired two years prior. She paused briefly when she spotted me, her scrutinizing eyes pierced me. She shopped for a while when I noticed she began making her way to my cash register line. *"Oh, my goodness, no, not my line!"* My one year of cash register confidence vanished and headed south like a wilted daisy. The scared, insecure little girl bubbled quickly to the surface as Helga inched her way closer. I smiled at each customer, handed them their bags of groceries, thanked them cheerfully, and I greeted the next. I rung items fast and professionally, all while Helga watched and scrutinized me.

My mind went blank when she pushed her cart heaped with groceries right to my register. I attempted a nervous smile and began ringing her items up as fast as I could. She didn't utter a word, not one single word, she only glared at me. When I told her the total, she paid and left, and I breathed a huge sigh of relief! A few minutes later, she returned to the store causing a scene and demanding to see the store manager, all while she waved her receipt in the air. My nightmare returned, I worried, *"My goodness, she's like a nightmare, why does she treat me so horribly?"* I wondered, while my stomach tightened into knots. Jane finished with her customer and asked, "Can I help you?"

"Yes, you can help me," she spoke loudly enough for all to hear, as she turned and pointed at me. "She over charged me, and I know she did it on purpose!"

Mortified, I couldn't believe what I was hearing. Because I was so anxious to get her out of the store, I accidentally charged her ninety-nine cents rather than the sale price of seventy-nine cents for three boxes of brownie mix. So, Jane cheerfully handed her sixty cents.

Helga looked at me before leaving the store and barked loudly for all to hear, "I'll never shop here again."

A few of my loyal customers made comments to Helga, "Good, don't come back." They smiled at me with care in their facial expressions.

Jane came up to me with concern in her voice and asked if I was okay.

I replied a frazzled, "I think so."

She then spoke a few words that relieved me immensely. "My God, she's such a bitch!"

Now, as I write these words, I find myself wondering, how is "Helga"? Has she overcome her anger? When I was eighteen years old, I had no clue why she was so cruel to me. Now, I'm fully aware of the demon she was fighting, and its ugly name is, *Jealousy!*

I loved working at the pharmacy, in fact, I worked there for nearly three years; they became my extended family. Therefore, I was greatly shocked the day I was fired! I couldn't believe my ears. Her husband Chap one of the owners had given me five raises and always spoke highly of me.

"What did I do wrong?" I asked.

Maddy, Chaps wife, the other owner, spoke curtly, "You're late to work a lot, and call in sick too much."

She was right. I was late a lot and called in sick far too often. Some mornings were harder for me to get up when I had cried myself to sleep the night before. There were various reasons. Some of which were, being kicked out of bed if I was too tired for sex. Other times, I didn't go to work because of bruises that couldn't be disguised. I became tired of disguising bruises, and at times, it was humiliating facing my workmates. Maddy and Chap had no idea what went on behind closed doors.

Her news devastated me. It was as if my only family shut the door on me! "Couldn't you give me a warning," I pleaded, through tears.

Her answer was "No!"

I blurted out awkwardly, "Steve hurts me!" She looked at me for a fleeting moment with compassion, but her answer was still "No!" Later, I found out from different sources that she too had been jealous of me (there's that ugly word again). Our sales man, Harold, came every two weeks to work on the advertisement. I saw them several times kissing and flirting with each other. In fact, every one of the employees knew that he and Maddy were having an affair; I believe her husband Chap was aware of it too. At times, I'd be in the back labeling and pricing store items and he'd flirt with me, she walked in on him flirting with me a few to many times. It wasn't till later, one afternoon, one of our great customers, and nearly the town Mayor kind of guy, told me how much he misses me not being at the pharmacy anymore. He also told me, "you are aware that she's insanely jealous of you? She wants to be the only Queen Bee. His words hurt my ears. To think that her jealousy fueled her to action was so unfortunate, after nearly three years of working with them, they had all become like family to me.

Early Signs of Trauma

I had begun to find gray hairs at age twenty-three, which was unusual because my mother and father never had gray hairs until their fifties. Signs of nervousness would unexpectedly take over my body, causing tremors which gradually worked their way from inside out—a terrifying feeling, mainly because it had its own agenda and I was not able to control it. It was like an earthquake, there was no way of stopping it; you simply rode it out.

Valium

As I had mentioned earlier, Steve was an only child and his tyrannical ways were only fueled when he didn't get his way, which meant compromising, which had also been the usual "norm" in my life. For instance, Steve decided to enroll himself in public speaking at our Kingdom Hall. This meant he would go on stage and conduct a five-minute Bible discourse on a chosen topic.

Public speaking was an enormous challenge for Steve; even when he'd share a comment from his seat, he would panic! This, in turn, required my attention. He'd nudge me, which was my clue to rub his shoulders, helping him to relax. He would be upset if I didn't massage his shoulders correctly. One time, I was taken aside by an elder asking me to stop causing a public scene. "You're always massaging Steve's shoulders," he reprimanded. And of course, I couldn't make a defense and explain what I was doing.

One day, Steve told me to make a doctor's appointment. "I want you to tell the doctor you have irritability problems. Tell him you get really bitchy around your cycle and that you'd like him to prescribe Valium."

"Why are you having me do this, Steve? None of it's true. I'd be lying."

His sharp-edged reply was, "It's the only way I can speak on stage."

I remember the doctor's reply the following week. He lowered his head and his bifocals slid to the ridge of his nose as he viewed me with question in his eyes. "You don't strike me as having irritability issues... Hmm... Well... If you say so." He then wrote me a prescription, and Steve had his drug to assist him in public speaking.

Back to Work

In time, Steve allowed me to go back to work. Even though my body and mind were weak, I desperately needed a daily escape into another world. I began working as a teller for a major bank in Saint Helena. I had never drunk coffee before because I didn't like the bitter taste; however, I found a little cream and sugar did the trick. I soon found myself drinking an enormous amount, as all the tellers did in order to keep up with the frenzied pace. I drank coffee instead of water, which was dehydrating my system and exacerbating my nervous condition. My manager was a slave driver. Never! Never! And I do mean never! Let her catch you walking! If you ran to your station tripping in your heels, she smiled and gave an approving nod, and sweaty armpits received a guaranteed thumb up!

Regardless of her tough whip-cracking work ethics, she was a pleasant person. She wore her hair pulled back into a tight ponytail, which drew my attention to the brown mole on her chin, which had one long wiry hair growing from it. Anytime she spoke with me, I avoided the mole calling to me. Oh, how I wanted to take tweezers and pull. Oddly, she wore the same polyester floral print dress every day. I visualized her at home, in front of the washing machine. She lifts her dress to her nostrils, inhales with deep satisfaction, her five days of slave driving!

I left that job after only eight months and transferred to a savings and loan. I was slowly being groomed for bank manager. I went from working as a teller to eventually having my own desk and working in the loans and savings department. I continued drinking copious amounts of coffee, until the day when everything went mental haywire on me. I helped a husband and wife open a savings account for $350,000. And a checking account for $5,000. They also wanted me to open two separate retirement accounts with $10,000 in each. In addition to that, I was opening a safe deposit box and issuing them teller cards. Multitasking at a frenzied pace was my norm; in fact, I loved the challenge and became quite good at it. However, midway through the transactions, I started having an anxiety attack. My heart raced at a frightening pace; I couldn't breathe nor was I able to think. With absolutely no forewarning, my brain went blank. It was as if someone reached down and unplugged me. A rush of panic crushed in on me. My head and hands went clammy and my blouse stuck to my perspiring back and chest.

I knew I couldn't freak out in front of my clients, so I excused myself, went to the bathroom, and splashed cool water on my face. I returned to my desk, attempting a composed state, and sat staring at my computer screen, as though I was staring at it for the first time. *What am I going to do?* I panicked, and looked at the couple, and then asked them if I could give them a receipt for the money and finish opening the accounts later. They looked at me as though they thought, *Is she crazy? Give us a receipt?*

I excused myself a second time; by the third time of excusing myself, the room swirled around me and everything went hazy. I started to faint as I grabbed onto the counter. I told one of the girls she would need to take over. I entered our break room (no pun intended), and broke! One of the girls followed me in and placed a call to my doctor. A nurse that dealt with trauma patients spoke soothingly to me and asked me a series of questions. Was I on street drugs? No. What about prescribed meds? No. Have you been using any in the past? No. My answers remained consistent. She walked me through my fear and explained to me that I was suffering from an anxiety attack. She spoke with me for nearly an hour, using visualization and breathing techniques to calm my body and mind. She made an appointment for me to see my doctor (not the same doctor I lied to for Steve) the following day. He, of course, wanted me to take Valium. However, because of my no drugs policy, my answer was no.

So, what did I do? I learned to live with the early stages of anxiety. My health needs were put on the back burner and I continued charging through life with absolutely no thought. Anxiety attacks became a regular part of my life, as my nervous system slowly headed towards a terrifying and critical point! I felt as though I needed to be scraped off the ceiling each time someone entered the room unexpectedly. When I'd lay down to rest, my eyes fluttered quickly. No matter how hard I tried to calm my eyes, they continued fluttering impatiently. I held my lips tightly pinched together like a prune while scrunching my brows together. My heart raced every night as though I'd completed a marathon. One or two times a week, I'd awaken from a deep sleep feeling terrified and paranoid. I never discussed these frightening symptoms with anyone. Steve's uncaring, abusive ways continued without let up, while I spiraled deeper and deeper into a frigid frozen state.

I started doing odd things, which had me alarmed. Rather than placing things back in the fridge, I was putting them in cupboards. One day, I searched for a two-pound block of cheddar cheese and found it spoiled a week later in my desk. I startled easily and would scream out in terror as though someone were attempting to murder me. Every nerve in my body burned with a hot electric sensation. Whenever I was hurt or someone startled me, I'd see brilliant colors flash before my eyes and a feeling of fire and electricity shooting out the top of my head and all ten fingers tips simultaneously. Sadly, I added this frightening new sensation to my overflowing pot and placed it on the back burner to deal with another time.

Our New Home

Steve bought a large corner lot in Saint Helena in the country, off Zinfandel lane, and my Father and Brother Luke built us a home. It was a family effort. Clark, Steve's Dad, designed a simple affordable home. We all shared in the work. We laid tile, we helped with the electrical, we painted, we ripped the siding off our foundation—wow, what a tedious job that in particular was.

And, six months later, we moved into our new home.

Mount View Hotel

Over the years, Steve had gotten used to receiving nearly my entire paycheck, so he approved of my next job, even though it was twelve miles away. We had been married seven years. It was the first time in our marriage that I felt free! I finally got to drive to work rather than walk. I absolutely loved working for the Mount View Hotel in beautiful downtown Calistoga. My spirit felt at home and seemed to soar like an eagle. I loved the people and the down-to-earth qualities everyone seemed to have. The Native Indians called Calistoga the healing place—they sure knew what they were talking about.

Summertime in Calistoga was the most exciting! Tourists came from distant parts of the world to eat at some of the finest restaurants, or to catch sight of the old faithful geyser, experience heavenly massages and detoxify in the famous mud baths, hiking the foothills leading to the palisades, and viewing the lava rock formations. And last, but definitely not least, they visited the most amazing wineries!

Getting ready for work was a sensuous ritual for me. All employees wore only black and white. I slipped into my black skirt and crisp white blouse, along with black nylons and heels to match. I walked out the front door, got into the car, pulled out of the driveway and breathed in the sweet air of freedom. A lightness filled my heart and a giddiness had me smiling all the way to work.

The Mount View Hotel was built around the turn of the Century and decorated of that period. The front entrance had elegant etched glass doors. When I walked through those glass doors, I felt I'd entered an era that time had overlooked, truly magical.

The breeze carried in the scent of roses and gardenias from the outdoor gardens. 1920s music flowed through the main lobby, restaurant, and bar. The deep mahogany floors gleamed from regular waxing. Two enormous fireplaces were on each side of the lobby. They rested during the summer months, and during the long, wet winters, they crackled and popped for tourists to warm their hands and backsides. During the summer, live music played in the bar on Friday evenings. The front doors were opened, which allowed the joyful melody to flow into the streets. My Spirit came alive each day I entered those etched glass doors.

A popular television series, called the *Falcon Crest*, was being filmed nearby, so it wasn't unusual to see the stars from the cast parading about.

One afternoon while I walked Main street on my lunch break, the movie called *Hot Rod* was being filmed. Crowds of people watched the production. I squeezed in to see what all the commotion was about.

The movie director spotted me in the crowd. He came up to me and asked if I'd like a role in the movie. "The pay would be minimal," he said. "Oh and do you know how to roller skate?" He smiled.

I was freaking out with excitement and anxiously replied, "Really? Yes, I'd love to, and yes I do know how to roller skate!"

The director gave me his phone number and asked me to call him.

Later that evening, I asked Steve if I could be in the movie. His answer was short and sweet— more like, quick and sour— "No!" Steve had our elders from the Kingdom Hall explain to me why I should not be in the movie; "It could lead to possible sin. Steve told you no and we support his answer to you, he's the head of your household, its important you obey him." They informed.

So of course, I complied with Steve and the elders.

Every day I worked away from home, I felt a new sensation growing within me. Almost as if I were discovering the feeling of freedom beginning to take root within my heart! Steve wasn't certain he wanted me working for the hotel anymore; however, he'd gotten used to my paychecks, so he still let me.

Freezer

Steve's abusive ways hadn't changed; I continued studying his mood swings, to determine if I needed to cautiously walk through the field of landmines or avoid walking near him altogether. He still masterfully hid his abusiveness from others.

One afternoon, I came home after work and Steve was in one of his serious moods. So, I knew it would be a landmine day, and to avoid any potential confrontation with him, straight to my bedroom I went to get out of my work clothes. I heard him ranting in the kitchen, "Oh, my god, what a mess!" Unlike the first year of our marriage when I had no desire to keep the house clean due to extreme depression, I kept the inside and outside of our home obsessively clean, to a fault, merely for the sake of appeasing Steve and eliminating any reason for him to attack me. I'd vacuum twice a day, and make sure everything was picked up and in order always.

What's he upset over? I thought. "Aubrianna, get in here!" he demanded. Perplexed, I entered the kitchen where he stood before the open freezer door, "There's spilled ice cream in here!" he growled.

"No, there can't be." I calmly said,

He grabbed a handful of my hair and shoved my head into the freezer, while he yelled with rage, "Can't you see it? What do you call that?" I couldn't see anything because my face was pressed against a frozen bag of vegetables. He gave my head one final shove and walked out.

My legs went limp beneath me. Pulling my head out of the freezer, I stared blankly at one tiny drop of chocolate ice cream. I feared Steve and his unpredictable rage, if only I could have screamed out my frustration, I would have said, "You're a horrible person, I want a divorce!" However, the Jehovah's Witness sermon echoed its prison sentence in my head: **God hates a divorcing! God hates a divorcing!** So, I continued as I'd always done, which was to stuff my feelings down into the pit of my stomach.

Chapter Twelve
God Hates a Divorcing

A group of young men from Italy came to Napa Valley to join in an International cyclist race. The Mount View Hotel hosted a welcoming party for the cyclists from Italy. I prepared our banquet room. The manager informed me that I would greet our guests and serve champagne, they told me, that even I could indulge in the giggly liquid myself. I had never tasted champagne before, my body enjoyed the sensation as the cool bubbles tickled my throat with each sip. I greeted and poured for the gorgeous men from Italy. I was amazed how they could dress in blue jeans, white t-shirts and look deliciously sexy and self-assured! Their broken English and dark yummy eyes had me feeling breathless. One man stood out from the rest. His name was Michael, he was intoxicating, with shoulder-length wavy dark hair and a smile that left me gasping!

Later that evening and off duty, I slipped out the back door and out of my high heels. While I walked in the direction of my car, I smiled and observed lovers embracing and dancing on the sidewalks, their bodies swaying to the sounds of live music overflowing from the bar and into the streets. Lovers held glasses of wine and strolled the streets.

The warm night air carried past me a gentle breeze, smelling of fresh cut lawn and sweet-scented gardenias. I stopped, closed my eyes, and breathed in the euphoric scent. The sweet sensations of the day delightfully settled into my heart. When I opened my eyes, there, standing before me, was Michael. "Ciao, Bella." My legs nearly buckled. He asked me in his sexy voice if I would show him around the town. Innocently, I responded, "Really? Well, no I really can't, I need to get home."

His eyes looked disappointed, he said, "No? Maybe just a little tour?"

My feet hurt, and I was tired; however, his presence had me feeling rejuvenated. I felt because he was a guest of the hotel, and I was the host, it should be okay. So, I gave Michael a barefoot walking tour of Calistoga. Twenty minutes into his tour, he asked if there was a nearby park, so I could rest my feet. I was touched by his kindness and concern for my feet. (of course, my innocence had me thinking, "Ahh how sweet, he's worried about my feet.")

Moments later we sat on a bench, under a crepe myrtle tree, our faces softly lit from a distant street light. With absolutely no forewarning, he leaned in and kissed me with gentle yet firm passion. Surprisingly, I didn't push him away. His delicious mouth and tongue had me reeling, euphoria ignited my body! *Oh, my god, where have these lips been all my life!* My thoughts raced!

He pulled slowly away from my starved lips and spoke four words, "Can I f***k you?" Cinderella's bubble burst and reality quickly set in. *"Can I f***k you?"* I silently and with warning thought.

"Oh, my god! No! I'm married." I informed him.

"It doesn't matter, Bella," he whispered, while enticing me with his amazing lips again.

My loins had never responded or longed like that before. I pulled away from his hypnotic lips and stood up as my head whirled with a delicious rush. I knew I needed to leave the situation or I'd have regrets. He quickly followed on my heels. I had nearly reached my car, when he asked if he could see me again.

I found myself absently saying anything just to shake him off me. "Yes, okay."

"I'm staying in Rutherford. I'll be back tomorrow," he said.

I jumped into my car and drove home and slipped safely into bed besides sleeping Steve. I had difficulty falling asleep; I tossed and turned, eventually lying flat on my back and staring up at the ceiling. I tried assuring myself that all will be okay. He'll be leaving for Italy as soon as the race is over. However, I had one enormous challenge to overcome: I couldn't stop thinking about those gorgeous brown eyes and delicious lips!

Four o'clock the following day, I entered the glass doors to work. I went about my jobs in my usual fashion, taking dinner and hotel reservations, making change for the waiters, with our impressive antique cash register, and delivering room service.

Each time, that magnificent Italian entered my mind, I swept him out, over and over again.

I stepped outdoors for my break and seated myself on a bench overlooking the main street of Calistoga. People watching was something I had always enjoyed doing. I watched as a steady stream of men, women, and children of all shapes, ages, and sizes passed me, when off at a distance, headed my way, was the gorgeous one!

He noticed me and his pace quickened; a moment later, he sat beside me. "Bella." He smiled and asked in his sexy broken English when I was getting off work. My heart pounded.

"Eleven tonight," I breathlessly whispered.

"I'll come back, and we will talk." Despite the magic he had over me, I nervously found myself wanting to shake him off again. "Bella?" he spoke.

"When I come back, can I f@%& you?"

I gasped nervously at his blunt crudeness, and corrected his speech, "Can we make love?"

"Si, can we make love?" Then in broad daylight, right there on Main Street, he kissed me, and my lips obeyed his delicious command. Gently he pulled away from my mouth and held my face tenderly in his hands. He guided my chin up so my eyes were level with his and asked again, "Bella, make love?" A choking pressure grabbed my neck, but I chose to ignore it.

The trusting, naïve girl wanted to scrape him off again, however I blindly blurted out with no thought of my consequences, "Yes."

He smiled and said, "Ciao, Bella," and walked away with a spring in his step.

I sat on the bench staring blankly at the pavement. *Why couldn't I have just said no to him?* I thought about devising a plan to get off work early. *But I told him yes. Oh, my goodness, what am I going to do?*

As I write this today, I understand a man or woman who's never been psychologically or physically abused may find it difficult to comprehend and fully grasp this "state of mind." In my case, my fear, was in saying the word "No", and especially saying No to a man. This feeling ran deeply within my core. I was always to obey a man, otherwise there were severe consequences. I had absolutely no clue of what healthy boundaries were, and I had no idea how to communicate my words. Sadly, because I told this man yes, I believed I had to follow through.

He strolled through the open doors with keys in hand at 10:40PM, smiling his bewitching smile! Once again, I ignored the choking sensation gripping my throat. Thirty minutes later, he walked me to his blue two-door Mazda.

The car was small inside and our shoulders practically touched. His cologne intoxicated my senses. We drove down Silverado Trail. *"Okay,"* I thought, *"this is ridiculous, the guy even drives sexy!"* He pulled into a long, winding driveway off Silverado Trail. My nerves kicked in, I shook with fear and apprehension. *What am I doing?* He brought the car to a slow stop and turned the ignition off. My body went rigid and my mind relentlessly nagged me, *"I told him yes, so I have to. I can't say no or he'll be angry with me."*

He stretched back in his seat looking somewhat perplexed, "Aubrianna, you look like a scared rabbit." He held my face with his warm hands and kissed me; his magnetism slowly melted away my icy fear. With no hesitation, he removed his jeans and underwear revealing his desire for me. He began kissing me while reaching under my skirt. He pulled down my stockings and underwear without detaching his warm full lips from mine. His passion was unnerving. He pulled away briefly to ask, "Make love, Bella?"

My Jehovah's Witness sermon swirled, around and around in my head. The only way out of marriage is: **Death or adultery! Death or adultery!** But... I'll be free! My lips whispered a guilty reply to Michael, "Yes." However, my conscience wouldn't allow me the indulgence of enjoying pleasure for the first time.

Michael's body shook with undulating desire and my mind reeled with guilt, shock, and relief simultaneously.

I'm free! I'm free! I'm free! A feeling of lightness surrounded my heart while Michael drove me back to my car.

"Aubrianna, I want to see you again."

I didn't answer him while I continued kissing him. He laughed, "Bella, si?"

Enthusiastically, I blurted out in between kisses, "Yes, Yes, Yes." His approving smile radiated through me.

I drove home and crawled into bed. When I awoke the following morning the lightness in my heart was replaced, with a heavy blanket of guilt.

That afternoon, I walked through the glass doors, and to my work station. My stomach was in knots, and I felt guilty beyond words. My time slot card had two messages from Michael, stating he wanted to see me, and that he'd be in later. Samantha, one of the girls I worked with, nudged me. "What's going on, Aubrianna? Is Michael from the welcoming party? That dreamy Italian dude? Well technically they're all pretty dreamy." She said with a mischievous twinkle in her eyes. Her twinkle soon left, when she noticed the color drained from my face; and the look of terror in my eyes, I felt as though I might vomit. "Oh, my God, baby, what's wrong?" I couldn't respond. I knew, that no one outside of my religion could possibly understand what was going on in my mind. I numbly worked throughout my day, while fighting back the nausea and heaviness in my heart. My mind raced terrifying thoughts, which wouldn't leave my head alone: "Aubrey, you're going to die at Armageddon. You're going to be dis-fellowshipped and you won't be able to see your family anymore."

Midway through my shift, Michael unexpectedly walked up to my work station. I couldn't breathe while thoughts nervously raced through my head. Observing, Samantha said, "Go baby, I'll cover for you."

Michael and I found a private spot to sit.

"Aubrianna, I want to see you again."

"I can't see you. I'm afraid! I'm really, afraid, Michael. I don't know what my husband's going to do. He beats me, and I have to tell the elders in my church what I did."

"Bella, come with me to a party tonight in Rutherford. We will talk more, don't go back to him. I leave home to Italy in five days. I want you to come home with me," he reasoned.

"You want me to go to Italy with you? You mean run away?"

"I won't let him hurt you, Bella. I'll be back to pick you up after work and take you to the party."

"Okay," I meekly replied. I couldn't say no to his face. *Why is it so difficult for me to say no?*

He kissed me tenderly, then stared caringly into my eyes, "I'll see you soon." He gently said.

Michael was completely unaware, that he would never be seeing me again.

No! I Can't Go Back!

My manager let me off work an hour early. I got into my car riddled with guilt, while contemplating my decision. Then, with no hesitation, I pulled out of the Mount View parking lot, drove two blocks and when I came to the four-way intersection, rather than turning to Saint Helena, I turned right, in the direction of Healdsburg and drove to my parents' home. Mom and Dad had moved since Steve and I had married, into a beautiful home my father built in the foothills of Fitch Mountain.

I sat nervously upon the enormous, comfy white sofa in the entertainment room, overlooking the soft glow of city lights below. Mom entered the room with a glass of Merlot. She handed it to me, "Drink this darlin', it'll calm you." I sipped the deep garnet colored wine as it warmed my throat and chilled bones. Tears slowly flowed as I spoke awkwardly between gasps. Mom gradually heard the whole story as I relieved my guilt and fear.

Her questions came the following day. Did he use protection? What if you're pregnant? And then the dreaded words came, "You need to talk to your father and eventually the elders, sweetheart."

Sheepishly, I went to my Dad explaining everything. Dad was outraged that Steve had been abusing me. "Why I'd like to take a two-by-four to his head," Dad gave me the typical elder's advice. "You need to call Steve and let him know what happened, then call one of your elders."

I called Steve as Dad instructed, "I'm so sorry for hurting you, Steve. I never wanted to hurt you." His tone was not angry; it sounded more like disbelief. I next called Elder Dean. He said he'd call later with an appointment for the entire committee of elders to meet with me along with Steve.

My religion is strictly a male dominated Patriarchal society, wise women have no part in elder committee meetings. Therefore, the advice they give, lacks the compassionate wisdom of the feminine; which essentially means it lacks heart and soul, it lacks balance.

Generally, three to five elders are present for a committee meeting. You're basically in a church court. They determine whether you're guilty or remorseful and this is decided after long, grueling hours of questioning. A person is questioned at several pre-arranged meetings; it's not over in one session, and each session can be hours long. They want to hear all details, and I do mean, all details! Don't even think of leaving anything out, I also feel without a doubt, some of those elders were getting aroused by the conversation.

If the verdict is guilty, you're excommunicated (dis-fellow-shipped) from the congregation. What this means is that no one can look at you or speak to you, including your biological family. When members of the Kingdom Hall see you headed their way, they quickly shift their gaze elsewhere and walk in a different direction. It happens on the streets, in the grocery store, in restaurants, anywhere. You're treated as if you're diseased. This form of discipline is designed to have the individual repenting, merely to gain his or her family and friends back.

What happens if you're not dis-fellow-shipped? An elder makes an announcement before the congregation giving the sinner's full name and informing everyone in a roundabout way of your misdeeds! What does this mean? It means they're not allowed to hang out with you; you're considered "bad association." Either way you look at it, you are marked with a scarlet letter!

The following day at my parents' home, I sat outside on the deck, overlooking the country side below me. The penetrating rays of the sun soothed and comforted me. I called the hotel and spoke with my boss Elaine. She told me Michael had called several times asking for me; she asked if it would be okay to give him my parents' phone number. A sinking feeling entered my heart; I knew he'd come by to pick me up for the party last night.

"No, please don't give him my parents' number, Elaine."

"Are you okay?" Elaine asked.

"I wouldn't expect you to understand, Elaine. My religion makes it far too confusing."

"Aubrianna, we can't lose you; you're vital to us. Do you need a few days off to sort out what's troubling you?"

"Yes! Oh, thank you, Elaine, thank you so much!" I responded.

Meanwhile, I continued to stay with my parents and Steve called daily asking if we could get together. My answer stayed consistently awkward, while crying into the receiver, "I don't know. I'm too confused."

Elder Dean called me with a date and time to meet at the Kingdom Hall in Calistoga. So, the following day, Mom parked her black four-door Jaguar at the corner of Cedar and Pine in front of the Kingdom Hall. Opening my car door, I slid off the tan leather seat and stood hesitantly; my legs shook and felt too weak to carry me.

There, standing at a distance, was Steve, looking despondent! He approached me and asked if we could talk alone for a moment. I turned and looked for my mother's reaction; she said she'd wait in the car.

As we walked towards the Kingdom Hall, Steve grabbed me tight and started crying. He told me through muffled sobs, "It's all my fault, Aubri, I'll try and stop hurting you. I'll really work on it. Just tell the elders why you did it, they'll understand." "Put all the blame on me," he pleaded! I was speechless and stunned by his reaction. I entered the Kingdom Hall on legs barely able to hold me up. My feeling was that I wanted to be free from Steve, even if I had to go through shame and humiliation. I wanted to be free from him.

I walked into the main room where four somber looking elders sat and stared at me. They told Steve and I to be seated. Each elder asked me humiliating questions while they wrote down my answers on their note pads. I was not able to stop my legs from trembling; they shook fiercely! I hung my head in shame while awkwardly answering all their degrading questions. No, we didn't have sex more than once. No, I did not enjoy it? No, we did not have oral sex. No, I haven't seen him again. Etc. Etc. Etc.

One elder—we'll just call him Larry—was determined to drive home his point and he most assuredly got a charge out of being in control; let's just say he had a lot of ego!

He had a reputation, of consistently looking at my breasts, and he was blatant about it.

He looked at me, with a smirk on his face. His penetrating eyes never left mine, (not even to look at my breasts) as he enunciated each word, drawing them out, to make his egotistical point.

"DID NOT BELLS GO OFF IN YOUR HEAD? DO

YOU NOT THINK?" he barked! (My mother later told me she'd heard his ruthless comments from outside.)

One gentle and very caring elder named Russ said, "How are we to help you Aubrianna, if you don't let us know Steve has been mistreating you? You're always smiling and looking happy. You need to come to us."

"But, I can't. I'm afraid to. If I told you Steve was abusing me, he'd be angrier with me," I gently tried to reason.

Two hours had passed, and the elders hadn't reached a decision. They will call me for a second meeting within the next few days. They instructed me to pray for forgiveness and for Jehovah's blessing to be upon me for this grave sin I've committed.

I left the building and went home with my mother. Three days later, I was instructed to be back for the verdict. My mother tried easing my mental state while she waited outside the Kingdom Hall a second time. "Honey, they're just men. They put their underwear on the same way every other man does." I wasn't amused by her attempt at calming me. I had stabbing pains in my chest intermingled with asthma!

Nervously, I sat staring, my eyes wide with fear, at each elder speaking to me. The verdict from a firmly speaking elder was, "Steve has forgiven you for your misdeed of adultery, and he wants to take you back into his home." **Oh, my God, No! Please, I can't go back, I can't! I can't! Please, No!** I silently pleaded!

"As a collective of elders, we have decided to silently rebuke you." What this means is you're not allowed to make public comments nor talk of anything spiritually based. "We want to see you're having a repentant attitude. One way you can show your obedience is by being in the preaching work regularly and being at all five bible meetings a week. When we see you're doing this, we'll know you have the right attitude. Then, your privileges will be restored when we see fit. Do you understand?" They asked?

"Yes."

"Do you have any further questions?" "No," I responded numbly.

In a state of disbelief, I left the building and walked on trembling legs towards mom's car. I limply dropped onto the seat and stared blankly at her.

"Well," she asked, "what happened?" "I wasn't dis-fellow-shipped." "Oh, thank heaven," she sighed.

"The elders said because Steve has forgiven me, I have to go back to him. Mom, I can't. I'm afraid! I'm really afraid Mom!! He says he'll stop hurting me. But, will he this time? He's always said that to me. He's waiting in the truck for me."

Mom's reply was, "Now that the elders are involved, sweetheart, maybe things will be different." I held her tight, hugging her as though I'd never see her again and said goodbye as I closed the door behind me.

Trapped

Steve and I drove home together. He spoke in a low tone, "I want you to call your boss and tell her you won't be working there anymore."

Not only did the abuse continue, it became worse! He used the adultery as a tool to belittle and humiliate me even more. Steve was not one to abuse alcohol; however, he began drinking heavily. He insisted on knowing the size of Michael's penis and made me show him where on Silverado Trail the adultery took place. So, every time Steve drove by that part of the road, he'd make me feel guilty, as he looked at the driveway and then looked at me. It's as though, he kept the memory of it alive, as a control tool. Because he had a fascination to keep it alive, it meant he could never heal. Metaphorically, he deliberately kept it raw and painful by pouring salt into his wound every opportunity he had. It wasn't until my healing journey that I realized this was a classic power and control maneuver, as long as he kept it alive, he was able to punish me.

One positive was, I began communicating with the elders that Steve's abuse had not let up; and I ran to my parents for refuge regularly. He would call and tell me, "I'll stop this time, really, I will." I became a pendulum on a Grandfather clock: I swung back and forth for many, many, many years to follow.

My father put repeated calls through to the elders in my congregation, telling them my situation had not improved. They would drop in from time to time, asking us how we're getting along. They would ask Steve, "Has the abuse stopped?" His reply was usually the same, "Yes 'I'm working on myself." I was a lifeless shell of a woman with no voice to be heard. Silently, I sat wide-eyed out of fear and kept my mouth shut.

Broken Bones

One afternoon, I was reading my Awake magazine. One of the articles talked about women having scriptural permission to leave an abusive marriage. I couldn't believe what I was reading! I read it over again. I was shocked, for surely this was my way out! I called my mother to see if she had read the article. "Yes honey, I read it too. It seems to be new information."

After several years, I was beginning to get a little gutsier, without any hesitation I put a call through to one of our elders. A meeting was arranged for Steve and me. I brought my *Awake* article highlighted in yellow just in case my overly nervous mind went blank. I explained my situation and desire to leave the marriage. The elder listened intently to my reasoning.

He questioned me, "Has Steve ever broken any of your bones?"

I stammered with surprise, "What?"

"Has Steve ever broken any of your bones?" he repeated.

I couldn't believe what I was hearing! "No," I responded.

"You don't qualify for leaving the marriage. This article you're quoting from is talking about extreme cases of abuse, such as broken bones."

I was in complete disbelief. Steve, was not only severely abusive, he was psychologically abusive. He robbed me of my life, and the elders are still not helping me? Oh my God! I'll go crazy! I was faced with no choice, or so I thought. The lonely, dark cage grew darker, the door remained locked and the disheartened, abused bird lost nearly all her white feathers.

Chapter Thirteen
First Signs of Breakdown

Starved for love and respect. With no road map or guiding hand to assist me, I remained stuck in chaos! Was there a loving hand reaching out to me, all along? When an individual is so caught up in their abuse and perpetual victim beliefs, they're unable to disembark from the "drama train" of negative thoughts and patterns, which essentially create our reality, as we barrel full speed ahead into nowhere. If we continue holding tightly to our familiar pain and our familiar misery, we remain victims, and we remain powerless! When we're a victim, we don't realize there's help available that patiently awaits our call, which essentially, offers us a lifeline and enables us to break free from our cages! This lifeline resides within us and outside of us and it starts with the recognition of something far richer and rewarding. It is within this recognition that we began our early stages of transformation. Which is the understanding of Self-love, Self-awareness and Self-respect. So, yes there is a lifeline available to us, and awaiting our willingness to grab on.

What is this lifeline? It is our personal guardian angel, waiting for us to ask for guidance and help. However, the key is not just asking, but rather following through with the guidance and answers that most assuredly will come to us. Rather than feeling we are alone in this world, we began trusting in a higher power to help us.

Fatigue

Major fatigue had always irritated Steve, especially during his free time when he'd have plans for us to go somewhere which usually required getting up very early and coming home very late. He would be angry with me when I'd fall asleep in the car.

"I want to share this with you Aubrianna, wake up," he'd bark loudly. I tried with all my strength not to nod off. One day, he pulled the car over, got out and came to my side, opened my door and commanded with an irritated uncaring tone, "Get up, you're driving now!"

Because of my mental and physical condition, occasionally, I'd sleep in on a Saturday—I was working full time at a bank, and my body craved sleep. Not to mention, my nervous system was literally burning out at a rapid warped speed. So, recuperation was a must, however, sadly, I wasn't getting it. Steve always had plans and was annoyed I slowed him down.

One day, he came home from work and told me he had something that would help me. "It'll give you energy," he said.

"Really, what is it?" I inquired with hope.

He pulled a small clear plastic baggy with two white pills out of his jean pocket. He said, "If they work, I can get you more."

Even in my frazzled mental state, something within me screamed NO! He handed me a one of the pills. I observed it closely and asked what it was.

His reply had a slight nervous edge to it, "I don't actually know. It's just supposed to give you a lot of energy."

The voice in my head spoke firmly again. I went straight to the bathroom, dropped it in the toilet and flushed! "I can't believe you would give me drugs, Steve!"

He never responded and surprisingly, he didn't abuse me for flushing them, or telling him no. To this day, I'm grateful I listened to my higher guidance. In my state of mind, I easily could have become addicted to a seductive and powerful drug called speed.

A Deep Desire

Regardless of my "unplugged" emotional state, believe it or not, I longed to be pregnant. Children and babies loved me; I had a certain quality that enabled children or adolescents to approach me freely and feel trust. Regularly, I volunteered and helped members of our congregation who had children or babies. Mothers were known for passing me their babies when needing help, and I of course was grateful to intervene. Cuddling, cooing babies made my heart warm and fuzzy. I babysat children regularly, and innocently thought I could fill the empty void and lighten my heart. However, those opportunities were not doing the trick. The emptiness ran far too deep. Every particle of my soul and every fiber of my being longed to be a Mother.

Sadly, a crippling fear wrapped itself around me and gripped me with a strangling hold. Which was dying at Armageddon, because of the sin I had committed with Michael the Italian man. Having a baby was out of the question, Steve had always been opposed to it. Not to mention, Jehovah's Witnesses taught that, Armageddon could come tomorrow.

Chapter Fourteen
We Moved Again

One afternoon, while running errands in Calistoga, I noticed a job construction site. Homes were in the early stages of being built, and a couple of building sites were available. I raced to the real estate office to inquire within.

It was the first affordable and budgeted housing complex for Calistoga. The real estate agent showed me the blueprint specs and I was sold: as the expression says, hook, line, and sinker. I called Steve at work and told him of my discovery and told him we needed to act immediately, or we'd miss out on a golden opportunity. He told me to go for it.

So, I handed the agent a postdated check for two thousand dollars. The funny thing was that Steve and I were not looking to buy or sell, it was just one of those things where I happened to be in the right place at the right time.

So, we put our home on the market and sold it five months later; I acted as real estate agent, because I wanted to save Steve as much money as possible.

We moved to Calistoga. It was lovely, and only a four-block walk into town. Our new home was a large spacious two-story, with three bedrooms, and three baths.

Even though our home in Saint Helena was built from family effort, it was time to say goodbye to our sweet two-bedroom one bath home in Saint Helena.

Chapter Fifteen

Divorce

We attended our bible meetings and preaching work regularly. One day, a new person attended the Kingdom Hall. His skin and eyes were dark from his Mexican/Italian heritage. He had thick black hair and a natural muscular build. His steady confident gaze seared through me. My cheeks blushed warmly while I shyly pulled away from his brazenly hypnotic eyes.

His name was Samuel. He soon became Steve's close friend and dropped in on us several days a week. Samuel had the uncanny ability to lift me out of my mental quagmire. Nothing could get him down and he charged through life with a rare optimism. He was unaffected by other people's comments of what they may have thought of him. I couldn't help but have a crush on him, which in time grew stronger.

One Friday afternoon, while working at the bank, I noticed a long line of people quickly forming. So, I left my desk and opened a teller station to help relieve the other tellers. We worked at a rapid pace to deal with the Friday crowd. The grumpy customers became grumpier; the impatient ones tapped their shoes on the dark-tiled floor, while loud restless children ran around the bank insisting on lollipops and balloons, when in strides Samuel, wearing shorts, a summer tee shirt, and sandals—along with his famous ear-to-ear charming smile. My heart sped with excitement!

While he stood in line, he watched me waiting on people. His captivating eyes seared through me. I continued working as quickly as possible when he trumpeted loudly, "HI AUBRIANNA!" His voice amplified down the corridor.

My cheeks flushed as I returned his greeting, "Hi Samuel!"

Everyone standing in front of him turned to face the man with the enormous presence. "HOW ARE YOU DOING ON THIS FINE DAY?" He smiled his words at me. The room fell silent. Children stopped wiggling, while customers shot curious glances at the unusual man, and then back at me to hear my response.

My cheeks flushed more, "I'm doing great Samuel, thank you."

Samuel nudged the grumpy man in front of him and asked him, "ISN'T AUBRIANNA BEAUTIFUL?"

The man scrunched his face and viewed me through his spectacles, "Why yes, she's a beauty alright." The man nudged Samuel back and said something to Samuel, while they both chuckled.

Lake Tahoe

I will never forget the enchanting, magical feeling of a weekend in Lake Tahoe, California. Steve, Samuel, and I boarded the enclosed gondola at Heavenly Valley ski resort. Fifteen to twenty men were boarded as it slowly climbed thousands of feet up the snow packed mountain side; we passed spectacular ranges and saw stunning views of Lake Tahoe. It just so happened that I was the only female on board, which I found to be a little awkward and exciting at the same time. The gondola was ful of men from France, speaking their beautiful, poetic language. Samuel looked at me, while he grinned a mischievous smile. *"Oh no, what's he going to say now,"* I nervously thought.

He spoke to the men from France, "Do you speak English?"

Most the men replied, "Oui" and they translated to those that didn't.

"Wel , at the count of three, I want you all to yell at the top of your lungs, AUBRIANNA IS BEAUTIFUL! three times. And by the way, this is Aubrianna," as he pointed to me.

"Ahhh oui", they smiled.

I dicn't blush pink; I'm quite sure I turned a deep shade of garnet.

"Are you ready?" he inquired.

Steve's face held an expression of smoldering flames just under the surface. In unison, fifteen French men hollered joyfully, with smiling faces. "AUBRIANNA IS BEAUTIFUL!

AUBRIANNA IS BEAUTIFUL! AUBRIANNA IS BEAUTIFUL!" They cheered and clapped for me. And in that one, single, monumental moment, I realized I had fallen in love, for the first time in my life, with a man bearing the name of Samuel.

Confessions

One afternoon, Samuel called me and confessed his feelings to me. I expressed my extreme unhappiness throughout our marriage, due to Steve's physical and verbal abuse. "He hits you, really? Oh Aubri, please tell me it isn't true? I can't believe it."

"Most people would never know. He's good at disguising his anger. I've wanted out of my marriage for eleven years now, but I can't because the elders say, "No Divorcing!""

One Friday, I was busy working at my desk when I received a phone call from Samuel. "I had an accident with a chainsaw at work today." His voice sounded weak.

My heart leapt. "Oh, my gosh, what happened?"

"I just got out of the hospital. I have over a hundred stitches in my leg. The chainsaw cut clear through my muscle. I'll be using a crutch for a while."

"Oh, my goodness, are you hurting?"

"No, they gave me painkillers. I'm just a little sore. Can you come over tonight after work, Aubri?"

"Yes, yes, of course we can. I'll call Steve. Can we bring you anything?"

"Yeah, you can bring me a six pack, and a couple limes."

When I told Steve what had happened, he said he was tired and just wanted to turn in early. "I'll go, then. I won't be gone long."

I showed up on Samuel's door step with his favorite Corona beer and a couple of limes. He came to the door using one crutch under his armpit. For the first time, he had a nervous smile. I went to the kitchen, sliced the lime, and got us both a beer. He sat sprawled out on his sofa while I sat in a chair opposite him, and slowly sipped on the cool amber liquid, while he told me about his chainsaw mishap. My eyes were wide with astonishment and relief that he still had his leg.

"Aubr , would you come sit here beside me?" I sat on the sofa about four feet from him, and asked him, "Are you okay? What's wrong, do you need me to fix you something to eat?" He hoisted himself up and scooted right beside me and said, "No thanks, I'm not hungry." I felt the warming effect of the alcohol and was blown away at our body chemistry; just sitting beside him was powerfu . Looking at his leg and seeing how swollen it was made me feel emotional about his condition. I willed myself to not cry and fought back the urge.

"What's wrong, Aubri?" I hesitated to speak, while holding my head low. His voice softly radiated through my body. His fingers gently lifted my chin and his warm, caring brown eyes melted me, as he asked again, "Aubri, what's wrong?" I looked down again, so I wouldn't be pulled into his magnetic charisma. His fingers guided my chin again. I nervously stared into his eyes as he leaned in and kissed my trembling lips. We continued kissing. The sensation heightened, while we explored feelings that had been denied for over a year. He broke away from my lips and spoke firmly, "Come to my bed, Aubri."

He made love to me sweetly. It rained while our bodies were embraced. The familiar pains of guilt and fear engulfed me. Samuel instructed me as a father would a little girl, "We shouldn't tell Steve or the elders in our congregation; you need to go home, or Steve will wonder why you're still here." The guilt weighed a thousand pounds on my heart. Yet, I loved this man, and was trapped in a cage with no way out.

Nearly a week had passed. I never called or spoke to Samuel. My absentminded thoughts wondered while washing the morning dishes, they were soon interrupted by the ringing of the phone. It was Samuel, he asked if we could meet in Napa, he wanted to talk with me. "Okay," I said. So, the following day, I pulled up to the arranged meeting place. He was no longer using his crutch. He wore his leather jacket and his usual charming smile. He got into my car and he uncovered what was hidden under his jacket: which was a bottle of champagne. "I thought we could enjoy this together."

"Oh, how sweet of you," I blushed. "There should be a park nearby where we can find a bench." I said.

"I had a motel room in mind, Aubri."

"Oh," I shyly responded. *He must love me*, I innocently thought, *He wants to be with me again.* We drove to Petaluma and checked into a motel room at 4:00PM.

At 6:00PM, we checked out of our room. Samuel was hungry, so he searched for a fast food restaurant. We stood in line like cattle, looking at the neon sign above us, describing one thousand ways to eat a burger! Two girls were ahead of us; from time to time they turned around, trying to get Samuel's attention, regardless of the fact that Samuel and I were together, they flirted anyway. Samuel gave them his killer smile, and turned and said to me, "They're pretty." They batted their lashes and giggled for the magnet man, when an oily-faced kid speaking with a monotone voice interrupted, "Next person in line, please, can I take your order?" They ordered chili fries with extra cheese and large diet Pepsis. Again, with no respect for me, they turned around and waved to Samuel as they walked away with their orders. I got very insecure and was surprised he'd flirt right in front of me. *"How can he do this to me?"* My heart ached. I believed that because I loved him and that we'd had sex, that we'd run away together and live the "happily ever after" life. After all, that's what Michael from Italy had wanted.

Boy, was I wrong! There was one loud and blaring contrast that I painfully discovered! He was not in love with me. Tears came to my eyes while I desperately attempted shaking off my hurt feelings. Samuel looked at me and asked in his typical booming voice, "What's wrong with you?" "Nothing," I sniffed.

"Ahhh, I get it," he smirked. "You think just because we had sex, I won't look at other girls?" His brazenness mortified me. I wanted to bolt out of the restaurant like a horse on a race track.

When alone in the parking lot, I became the classic needy and clinging female. I held tightly to my hopes and dreams as I sobbed through our conversation. A veil of fog lifted, and my rose-tinted glasses were removed from my eyes. It now became crystal clear that his intentions were not what I had innocently hoped for.

I told him I couldn't live with our secret and that we needed to confront the elders. "No, we can't. I don't want Steve to know," he said. However, my conscience was far too sensitive and wouldn't allow me to leave it alone for the sake of not hurting Steve or avoiding the "Letter A" humiliation before the congregation.

Love Awakening

Many years later, on my mission of healing, I discovered within myself the need for severe discipline and humiliation, whenever I did even the least thing wrong! Why? Because from the age of two forward, I was punished severely.

I hadn't awakened to the understanding of this concept yet, and apparently, I had not experienced enough suffering either. When we're ready to end our misery, a stream of light settles gently upon our seed of understanding and takes root within our heart and mind. The Bible speaks of the truth that sets us free. I believe that truth to be, learning self-Love. The journey of Love can only start within us first. And, it is within this recognition, that we can begin the early stages of being set free! We cannot genuinely love someone outside of ourselves, if we don't understand the vitalness of self-love first.

Unfortunately, not everyone is ready to learn self-love. Some choose to remain in their so called familiar life of pain. And, some go deeper into despair by numbing their pain with addictive stimulants such as drugs, materialism, alcohol, cigarettes, eating disorders, sexual addictions, prostitution, gambling and so forth—all of which are distractions which deaden our authentic feelings, and drive us further from the truth that sets us free.

A Familiar Road

I was headed for far more emotional disaster than I could ever have imagined. All I ever wanted and desired, was for Steve to deeply love and care for me. I desired a complete immersion of love with a man. I had longed for a man to be my savior— "the one and only"—to love, rescue, and take care of me for the rest of my life. Was this man a figment of my imagination? Shall I burst your bubble with the truth? Yes! This man was most definitely an enormous figment of my imagination! That kind of man simply does not exist. And it's unfair to a man to have unrealistic aspirations of a Cinderella fairy tale life.

I drove to my parents' home as I'd done six years before. I was faced with déjà-vu all over again. Even though it was against our religion, my family still supported me in leaving the marriage. While home, Liz tried motivating me by taking me to the theatre. We saw *The Color Purple*. Oprah Winfrey, Whoopi Goldberg and Danny Glover stared in the movie. It was about a passive wife and a severely abusive husband. Liz's goal was to catapult me out of my dilemma. Despite my family's support, I was programmed to believe, that I was doomed for death at Armageddon! And, my co-dependent ways had become a drug to me. I vacillated between misery and debilitating fear, like the pendulum on a Grandfathers clock. When I shared with Steve what had happened, he surprisingly did not want me to leave him. Regardless of Steve's ten years of abuse, I deeply regretted causing him pain.

A week had passed, and I met with the elders as I'd done before. My nerves shook violently. Elder Larry was on my committee meeting again. He still enjoyed his games of twisted control. His eyes held mine and his words clearly etched in my memory as he once again enunciated each word loudly and clearly, "Did not warning bells go off in your head telling you this is a bad idea? Did you not think? You don't strike me as someone that doesn't think. But this situation has happened to you once before." He repeated his words a second time, "Did you not think?" I had a meltdown and sobbed uncontrollably as my mind took me deep into a pit of unexplainable pain.

After two separate meetings, the elders reached their verdict: I was not dis-fellow-shipped. I would show my repentance by always being out in the preaching work and never missing any of our Bible study meetings, which I mentioned before are five meetings a week. Congregations in other districts and counties announced my name to the members of each church so they were aware I was considered "bad association." I was not to share any personal comments at our public discourses, nor was I allowed to hang out with my friends. Again, most members treated me as if I had a disease. Incidentally, I was reproved for one year the first time, and two years the second; it turned out they had forgotten to do a follow up and remove my discipline.

One afternoon, I went to a health seminar with Liz. She brought along two female members from her congregation in Santa Rosa. Nancy treated me with love and compassion, but Ruth treated me unkindly the entire day. At one point, she told me to watch myself and stay out of trouble with her cold, reprimanding finger pointing judgment at me. I still had no voice and merely held my head low and responded with "Okay."

Samuel still attended the same congregation and he eventually married a beautiful woman a short time later. She eventually became pregnant and mothered two of his children. I envied her with aching in my heart. She not only married

Samuel, but also became a mother. The desire to be a mother still resided deeply in my heart. I felt experiencing the miracle of being pregnant and the joys of motherhood would heal the gaping hole in my heart.

Chapter Sixteen

I Can't Believe My Eyes

I was one of those women who never bothered keeping track of my monthly cycle; I knew I'd never be pregnant, so why bother? One morning, I felt different than usual. My breasts had a lot of veins just under the surface of my fair skin and my nipples were a slightly different color and were tender to the touch—it was nothing I'd experienced before. I mentioned these strange sensations to my sister Anne, who was the mother of a toddler girl named Malaya.

"Aubri! You might be pregnant," she said.

"Pregnant! Oh, my goodness, really?"

So, I purchased a pregnancy test kit at our local pharmacy. The cashier noticed my smiling face and said, "Good luck." The following morning, I walked to the bathroom as though I were partaking in a sacred ceremony. I sat down on the toilet, holding my breath as my heart pounded. If I was pregnant, it would show a plus sign and what I saw, was the most beautiful plus sign! *OH, MY DEAR GOD, I'M PREGNANT!*

Throughout the day, I wondered how I'd break the news to Steve. *We've been married twelve years, maybe he'll feel differently now.* I hoped he would be as joyful as me. When Steve came home from work, I asked, "Can we sit down, Steve? There's something I need to tell you."

We sat down; my face glowed!

"Well?" Steve inquired.

Awkwardly, I blurted out, "I'm pregnant!" My eyes sparkled, while I hoped for the same expression in his.

He looked at me with a blank, yet serious gaze, "What did you say?"

"I'm pregnant!"

He was silent; the pause lasted roughly a minute, and then he spoke, "I see." He got up off the sofa and walked out of the room.

For the next few weeks, I tried communicating with him and soon realized it was useless. He shut me out of his life by rarely speaking to me the entire nine months. Because this was the most important part of my life, I simply wouldn't allow Steve's "silent treatment" to rob me of the great treasure growing within me. I read *What to Expect When You're Expecting* from cover to cover twice, as though it were my Bible.

What made this time in my life more challenging was that my parents had moved to Oregon, so I didn't have my Mom to talk to about my pregnancy.

The nursery walls were neither pink nor blue, rather a clean and sanitary white. The room was decorated with one of my favorites: *Winnie the Pooh*! I sat down in the rocking chair and glanced at my surroundings. Everything was in place, even the changing table was stocked with cloth diapers ready to be filled! Knowing my baby had grown accustomed to my voice, I sang. (In fact, nearly all the nursery songs I sang were ones I created, which I would sing while rubbing my abdomen.) At times, I still had difficulty grasping the concept that I was pregnant.

It's a funny thing: when a woman's pregnant, her growing abdomen becomes public property. I'm sure all waddling, radiant mothers know exactly what I'm talking about. Strangers approach as though magnetically drawn to your belly, and they ask the question you've been asked, ten thousand times already. "Do you know what you're going to have—a boy or a girl?" And when they heard my reply of "No," they generally backed away with expressions of disbelief, as though I were foreign to them. "Why don't you want to know the sex of your baby?" Next came the flood of all the reasons why I should: You can prepare the nursery in pink or blue and pick out all the clothes ahead of time. These strangers, with their hands on my belly, looked at me as though somehow, they were helping me see the light of reason. As if I'd say to them, "Oh, my god, why didn't I think of that? Yes, of course, you're absolutely right." Instead, I politely stated my reason, "I don't want to know. I prefer being surprised." They soon departed, along with their sour lemon expressions.

I was also surprised by how women would gush on about their horror stories, in the delivery room, with no consideration of my fears. "Oh, my god, it's the most excruciating pain! Make sure you get an epidural."

Other comments seemed catty rather than caring, "Look how fat you're getting!" followed by laughter while they pointed at my pregnant belly. I walked five miles every day, mainly because I'd been told it helps the delivery go faster; I was anything but fat. Please, my fellow sisters... Try this one on for size: "Look how your baby's growing. You look so beautiful."

I found one comment the most offensive! I heard it from many mothers and read it in magazines. "When you put your baby in the crib, they're going to cry. Don't pick your baby up. Leave the room, close the door behind you, and ignore the cries. They'll eventually fall asleep on their own."

My personal feelings on this controversial and sensitive topic are: that our babies have been living in the safest, most nurturing environment for nearly a year! They've grown comfortably familiar with our voice and beating heart. On the eventful day of delivery, our babies are going through major trauma! When a mother is not mentally and physically prepared for childbirth, she naturally will scream out in agony! The baby hears its mother's screams, which frighten it even more. The mother becomes filled with adrenalin, which the baby in turn is also getting.

Your baby is then slowly squeezed out of its warm, comfortable home and brought into a new cold and uncaring world. If its umbilical cord is cut too soon, your babies oxygen supply is cut off, which forces it to breathe. Your baby is then hung upside down, generally by an uncaring doctor with a golfing agenda (not all doctors.) Then shocked with a hard slap on its naked bottom, taken away from its mother to be cleaned, weighed, and clothed.

Now I ask... How can a mother allow her baby to be taken away to the nursery? Our baby has abruptly been taken away from its home. I urge you mothers to take your baby to your breast and bond immediately. It is only a matter of communicating your desires to the nurse ahead of time.

Urgent Call

Steve and I were awakened from a sound sleep by the ringing of our phone at 2:30AM. The call was from my Mom. She cried through her words, she told me that my father had another heart attack, and that he was in the hospital! I felt frightened inside. I realized how precious life is and just how easily it can be taken away. Even though I knew the importance of being calm for Mom and especially for my baby growing within, I feared Dad might not see my baby. Rather than going back to bed, I packed my clothes.

Steve drove me to Santa Rosa and dropped me off at Liz's house. Liz, her boyfriend, and I drove to the San Francisco Airport, boarded the plane and landed in Oregon six hours after mom's original phone call. The doctor was scheduling open heart surgery for a triple bypass.

I opted to stay with Mom and help after my father's surgery. Daily, I changed his bandages and stayed busy doing chores my father ordinarily would have done, such as mowing the lawn, fertilizing, and so forth. Even though my mindset when living at home was the family "work horse," I found I was happier and healthier when I kept busy—which also had the benefit of keeping me in shape while pregnant.

I appreciated my time with Mom and Dad and they shared in my enthusiasm about my pregnancy. During my Dad's lengthy three-month recovery, I felt I had bonded with him for the first time. I realized we were alike in many ways. I was able to see his kinder, more sensitive side and admired his love of God.

I was nearly six months pregnant when I flew to Oregon and was close to full term. When friends dropped in to visit my father, they were surprised I was still there. One man had the nerve to ask me, "You must not be married then, huh?"

When I reached my eighth month, I was finally beginning to show signs of looking pregnant. It was important I got home and close to my doctor. My final weeks of pregnancy went slowly, I no longer had the emotional support of my parents. I signed Steve and me up for natural childbirth classes, but I walked into the first class with no husband to accompany me. I ached for a happy, supporting husband like the beautiful, waddling women had.

Steve began to show signs of interest and came to our second class. I was ecstatic! He opened and told me his fears of being a father. I found when I didn't fixate on our baby, he was okay. I couldn't expect him to change overnight and I was grateful he was finally talking to me.

Germs Haven't a Chance

Now in my ninth month, my projected delivery date was October twenty-fifth, which really doesn't seem to apply for first time moms who generally go two weeks past the due date. However, I felt that I would deliver earlier, rather than later, so my parents came down one week before the delivery date. Dad made it clear to me, "Honey, you'd better have my grandchild during the next two weeks," he chuckled. "If not, we're heading back home to Oregon." Having my parents there to help was a blessing. Because of my nesting instincts, I shampooed the carpeting throughout our home as well as the sofas. I felt an addictive need to find the one last germ hiding from me. There was only one person who could successfully wage the war on germs, and that would be... Mom. She pulled on her yellow rubber gloves. "Aubri Rose, one can never have enough rubber gloves," she would always say. And off she went with a bottle of bleach in one hand and a magnifying glass in the other (just kidding.)

Our large, spacious garage was nearly filled with bottles and cans in need of sorting and recycling. My mother, the drill sergeant, told Steve he needed to take care of the recycling. "Aubrianna shouldn't be doing this work," she complained.

Steve always had his own agenda. "Marilyn," he informed my Mom, "Aubri got this whole recycling bit started. I've always thought she should just throw it in the trash, It's easier. And besides, I'm busy after work. I need to work on my sports car."

I appreciated Mom trying to step in and have Steve shoulder some of the burden like most husbands. Regardless of her attempts and her fiery eye of disapproval, she soon came to realize she was dealing with a man of a different breed. Mom suggested we just place them all in large plastic bags and get them in the truck. "We can sort them out at the recycling center," she encouraged.

My Dad had the strength of an ox, even for a man that recovered from a triple by-pass surgery. During the next week, he completed all the accumulated handyman chores. He too, was not pleased with Steve's unwillingness to help. One afternoon he said, "Aubri Rose, I'm not one to pry into someone else's affairs, but you're my daughter and knowing Steve doesn't help you around the house with chores that require a man's help sure doesn't settle right with me."

He was right, I had become used to doing most everything myself. I remember a neighbor saw me working in my front yard. He slowed down his car, rolled down his window and said, "I gotta get my wife to see this!" I even had neighbors' wives say to me, "Would you please stop! You're making us look bad. Our husbands think we need to be doing what you do." I would vacuum the house twice a day about fifteen minutes before Steve would come home. I would nervously scan the house looking for any one item that was not put back in its place. For anyone that may have watched the thriller starring Julia Roberts: Sleeping With The Enemy. That movie described me perfectly.

Oakland Fires

October 22nd Three days away from my due date. It had been another freakishly hot day. It was 8:00 in the evening and practically every channel on TV had news coverage of the horrific fires in the Oakland hills. The heat from the flames was so hot it caused the oil within the eucalyptus trees to burst with a loud crackling noise before they were engulfed in flames, as were the homes. I couldn't watch any more devastation on the news, so I decided to go outside for a walk. We hadn't any rain yet, which saddened me, because Oakland could use the rain. I walked in a world of gray. Every parked car and all the bushes and rooftops were covered in ash. Ash gently fell from the sky carrying with it a silent, yet destructive memory.

I continued walking in the suffocating warm night air. I prayed out loud for rain to fall upon the cruel, unyielding fires, "Please refresh and quench the thirsty Oakland hills with water." I became overwhelmed with a deeply rooted, ominous sensation. I couldn't quite place a finger on it, but it brought me to tears.

Recycling Day

The following morning, October 23rd, I awoke early and got dressed for a busy day with mom and my sister Anne. Mom and I left in the truck loaded with recycling. We swung by to pick up Anne and head to my appointment with my midwife. Upon inspection, my midwife encouraged, "Aubrianna, you should probably go home and get some rest after your shopping, because from this point on you could really go into labor at any time." So, we drove to the recycling center, I was having strong cramps while driving, which had mom and Anne concerned.

We sorted through bottles and cans. Each time I experienced painful cramping, I would do as Native women have traditionally done: I squatted through each cramp and breathed deeply. When the labor pains subsided, I continued to sort. You can only imagine the strange looks I was getting from people: a woman in labor at a recycling center, squatting every ten minutes.

I was thrilled to have the heavy burden of recycling out of the garage. A meager check was handed to me, and off I drove us to lunch.

While Annie, Mom, and I sat in the restaurant, I continued breathing through cramps; the only difference was that they were progressively getting over-the-top painful. Mom and Anne exchanged concerned glances with each other and insisted on taking me back to the hospital.

I breathlessly said, "But she said for me to go home and get some good rest." We left the restaurant and I got into the driver's seat.

Mom spoke firmly, "Oh, no you don't. Aubrianna, you need to hand over those keys and sit in the passenger seat, now! We're going back to see your midwife." Reluctantly, I agreed.

We arrived back at the doctor's office. Mom, having had the experience of six births, told the nurse to contact my midwife and to put me in a birthing room now! We headed straight to the birthing room in my "lovely" hospital gown. My midwife entered twenty minutes later with a smile.

"I haven't made it home for the nap you wanted me to take," I stated

She examined me and said with a surprised smile, "You're dilated to four already. It's a good thing you didn't go home after all."

I had done extensive research on a variety of herbs native women took, enabling them to have quicker labor. What I wasn't aware of was, that the herbs essentially caused my contractions to be one on top of the other, each one peaked at maximum strength. Taking these herbs allowed my pregnancy to not only be on time but also caused it to be far more intense than I had anticipated. I wanted to have a drug free birth. So, I taught myself hypnosis and repeated my affirmation daily, which was: a quick delivery. Unfortunately, I left just one important piece of the puzzle out: *painless!* Oh, well, I guess that's one of those learn-from-experience, hindsight sort of things.

Another thing I had no advance knowledge of was that some mothers also experience back labor! This is when you simultaneously have unyielding, knife-stabbing pain in your back as well as the normal contractions—most definitely a double whammy! If I had screamed out due to the pain, it would frighten my baby more. So, what I did was breathe and breathe and breathe like I've never breathed before. I must say, giving birth naturally felt as though I was having an out-of-body experience.

Periodically, the nurses would check in on me and were surprised each time to see me coming along much faster than most first-time moms. Roughly three hours had passed when the nurse checked me again and said, "You're completely dilated! Do you feel an urge to push?" I couldn't physically feel anything because the pain was so intense. She told me to go ahead and push. Sadly, I took her advice; my baby's head had not dropped fully into delivery position yet. I pushed, and nothing happened. I pushed again, and still nothing. I bore down and grunted and pushed with such intensity, the blood vessels popped in my eyes. I felt something tear within my uterine wall. It was a far different pain than I'd grown accustomed to, but I remember thinking it was probably all part of the painful process, which it wasn't.

Nearly the entire time of bearing down I had my eyes squeezed tightly shut. I remember at one point opening my eyes for a moment. There must have been ten people standing in front of me, most of whom I didn't know. They stared at me as though I was on display at the local circus. I was mortified! And then, when I saw in the crowd my father-in-law, I was horrified! He stood there, looking between my legs! *Oh, my God, what a nightmare.* I couldn't speak but Steve saw me give him a fleeting expression of *Help!* He came to my side and I grunted through the contractions, "Please get everyone out."

A few minutes later, it happened again. I was humiliated beyond words! There, staring between my legs again were my Mother and Father-in-law and other people I didn't know. Did anyone hear me say: "Hey everybody, grab your popcorn and come on in. The admission is free". It turned out that my mother had hollered down the hall, "She's ready to push, come see the baby, everyone!" Steve ushered everyone out a second time.

Karma?

At 6:01PM, my baby was born: a beautiful boy! He weighed exactly eight pounds. His name was Maximilian. His hair was thick and wavy, and the color of mahogany brown. He was peaceful; he didn't cry as most babies do (at least not yet). I had instructed the hospital staff weeks beforehand, to bring him to my arms immediately, with his umbilical cord attached. I was going to bond with my baby, they could clean, dress, and weigh him later. He had large eyes, the color of dark chocolate, and long, tapered fingers. The nurse's comments were, "Oh, he's going to be a pianist one day with fingers like that! And his hair is so gorgeous. Did you ever see so much hair?" I tenderly spoke to my beautiful son, "I love you, little Maxi," and gently kissed his tiny forehead. He stretched his neck, tilting it upwards, and stared into me. I was looking into the eyes of an "old soul."

The midwife came in later to fill out Maxi's birth certificate. She asked me what time he was born.

I was so used to rounding off my numbers, I said 6:00 and that's what she wrote down. Anne said to me, "Aubri, he was born at 6:01. You'll change his Karma." My thought was, *Karma?* So... Just to set the Karmic record straight: even though Maxi's birth certificate says 6:00, the universal law recorded his birth time as 6:01!

When everyone left the hospital, I fell asleep. I was awakened by a nurse checking in on me. I asked,

"Where's Maxi?"

"Oh, we put him in the nursery, so you can rest."

I attempted sitting up and winced from the gnawing pain. It turned out I had a severe uterine tear because I listened to the advice of a nurse and pushed too soon. The nurse came to assist me.

"Here," she kindly said, "let me help you to the bathroom."

"Oh, I don't need to use the toilet. I'm getting my son."

"Honey, you'll spoil him!" she responded.

"Was he spoiled when he lived in me for nearly a year?" I kindly retorted.

I walked to the nursery. Maxi lay swaddled in blue, his eyes wide open, while babies screamed around him. The nurse looked at me with a question in her eyes and placed Maxi in the hospital stroller. I strolled the two of us back to my room and held Maxi in my arms and breast fed him, just as it should be.

On that evening, a second miracle happened: it began to rain. And, it rained and rained and rained. The parched earth was soon refreshed, and the Oakland fires were snuffed out.

Chapter Seventeen

Breakdown

My little Maxi had what a lot of babies suffer from: colic. He cried for nearly two years. I couldn't sleep at night because I held him, singing lullabies while I rocked him. He cried all day and cried all night. The circles under my eyes were deep and dark and it felt as though my eyes had sunk into their sockets. I craved sleep and considered it a luxury. I would go to the toilet and he sat on my lap, crying. When I bathed in the tub, hoping for peace, he'd scream! I felt my head would explode and I'd go crazy with insanity!

I tried every natural remedy for colicky babies. And when friends and mothers saw my zombie appearance, they all gave me the same advice, "Just let him cry it off. You need your sleep!" I couldn't imagine being in such pain alone without a loved one nearby to comfort me. This is my baby; it went against my grain to follow the recommended advice.

Then one day, the dark, heavy cloud of colic lifted! Because Maxi had gotten used to me being with him twenty-four-seven, when he'd wake up and I wasn't beside him, he would cry for me. My challenge was getting him to sleep without me present. I would gently settle him into his crib, tip toe out of his room, and crawl into my bed. My body was heavy with physical and mental exhaustion. When I'd close my eyes, I heard loud rushing sounds in my head and felt as though I were falling into the mattress. Just when the warm sedating feeling of sleep began to lull me into the dream world, I'd awaken to Maxi's cries for me. I stumbled as though drunk every night down the hallway into his room to console him and start the process over and over again. My average sleep was three hours a night, every night! The love I had for Maxi was unlike anything I'd ever experienced, which allowed me somehow to survive from little sleep.

Coughing Up Blood

One summer afternoon, Steve went outside to sunbathe in our backyard. I was concerned when I saw baby Maxi crawling behind him. Knowing of a baby's curious nature (they put everything in their mouth and decide later if it's worth keeping or spitting out), I asked Steve, "Please keep an eye out for Maxi."

"Yeah," he murmured.

Steve lay in the sun and baked his perfectly muscular body. He worked religiously in the gym a couple hours a day lifting weights, allowing him to sport a well-developed physique. Beads of sweat formed in each muscle's crevice as his tan deepened to a bronze.

I was busy in the kitchen and peeked out the window from time to time to check on Maxi. Roughly twenty minutes had passed, and he crawled back in through the open sliding door fussing and whining.

"You okay, little Maxi?" I asked while scooping him up to see what was bothering him. He continued fussing and started to cough. I held him in my arms while stepping outside to ask Steve if anything had happened.

Steve's curt reply was, "Stop bothering me!"

I went back into the house, thinking Maxi possibly needed a nap. He began coughing up blood slightly diluted with saliva. Anxiously, I walked outside still holding Maxi. "Steve, there is something wrong with Maxi."

"What!" he said, obviously annoyed his tanning hour had been interrupted with my ridiculous concerns.

"Maxi's coughing up blood. What should we do?" "I don't know!" he barked. "I'm sure he's fine. You're probably just overreacting." He settled back into his browning routine. His lack of concern upset me, and Maxi continued fussing.

Despite my fear of bothering Steve a third time, my motherly instincts kicked in. I went outside again and managed a somewhat commanding tone, "We're taking Maxi to the emergency room and if you don't come with me, then I'm going by myself."

Steve, not used to hearing me speak with authority, looked somewhat surprised! And to my amazement, he got up! However, because of his perfectionist ways, he wouldn't allow an emergency to affect his dress code. He took great pride in his appearance at all costs. For fifteen minutes, I sat waiting with Maxi in the car for prince charming to emerge in all his flawlessness!

The doctor was mystified; the x-rays were inconclusive as to what Maxi had swallowed. He gagged as the doctor reached far down into his throat with what appeared to be pliers. Maxi's face was red from crying. I held him in my lap, consoling him, "It's okay honey, the doctor is just trying to help you." The doctor's third attempt was successful. He pulled a foxtail out of Maxi's throat! It had managed to work its way deep into his throat.

"It's a good thing you brought him," the doctor said with a concerned tone, "Foxtails only work their way down, never up! It was headed for your baby's lungs. It could quite possibly have punctured a hole in one!"

Another frightening incident took place that same summer. Maxi was about seven months old, and I had filled a blue plastic wading pool for his enjoyment on hot summer days. Having the pool set up added another element of danger for an unsuspecting baby! The potential hazard would not allow me to let down my "mom guard."

It was early evening and Steve walked outside to prepare for our barbeque. Maxi once again followed on his heels. I asked Steve to keep a close eye out for Maxi because of the pool. I worked in the kitchen preparing a salad. A few minutes had passed, and Steve walked in the house. I continued to slice vegetables for another minute when I realized Steve had come into the house alone! I dropped the knife and ran outside to the wading pool. Oh my god! There was Maxi, floating face down in the water! I reached down, grabbing him out of the pool. His body was limp like a rag doll and he was not breathing! I held him in such a way that his head dropped forward as I patted him hard several times on his back. I silently hoped he wouldn't require mouth-to-mouth because I didn't know how to do it. He coughed and let out a gurgling cry as water and saliva bubbled out of his mouth!

Steve came out, asking what all the commotion was about? I said breathlessly through tears, "I asked, you to watch him and you didn't. I came outside, and he was drowning!"

Steve's annoyed reply was, "Oh, stop overreacting, Aubrey!"

I Need Sleep!

When Maxi was three years old, one of our favorite things to do, we called "musical fences." We'd each search for a long stick. When Maxi found one, he'd jump into the stroller and we strolled down the sidewalk past homes with wooden or metal fences. We'd hold out our sticks while I continued pushing the stroller; each slot made a slightly different tune. Maxi's face would brighten with enthusiasm. He'd giggle loudly and say, "Again mama, again."

When Maxi was three and a-half, he seemed to get his second wind at night. Steve was generally in bed by 8:00PM and his alarm sounded off at 5:30AM. Having him in bed so early meant keeping the house soundless. We didn't want to awaken the "sleeping giant," which brought back my childhood memories of my Mom's nonstop threats: "Sshh! Be quiet! Your father's sleeping!" after my father's first heart attack.

One evening around 11:30, Maxi's limp, sleeping body, finally gave up his resistance to sleep, and entered his dream world. My challenge was to quietly tip-toe out of his bedroom and not awaken my little prince, which required the speed of a turtle. One slow movement at a time, I stood successfully above his bed, while he slept peacefully.

Exhausted, and thinking of nothing but sleep, I walked down the softly lit hallway and into my bedroom; I crawled quietly into bed so as not to awaken Steve. Because my nerves had become severely rattled, it usually took an hour or more before my body would even consider the possibility of sleep. It was roughly 12:30, and I began to settle into a warm state of relaxation, when our bedroom door burst open and a flood of light poured in along with Maxi. My heart raced quickly again, and my nerves went jumpy. I lifted my heavy head from my pillow and squinted through weary eyes! Maxi toddled over to my side of the bed, and whispered, "Mama."

I dragged my sleep-deprived body out of bed and whispered to Maxi, "We can't wake up daddy, sweetheart. You need to go to sleep, it's late." After some time, I tiptoed back out of his room and crawled back into mine. It's now 1:00AM, and this typical scene repeats itself, as it does every night.

One evening, Steve grumbled, "Can't you get him under control?"

Maxi came running into the room, giggling, and I had what I call a meltdown; I pleaded through tears, "Please Steve, help me! I'm so tired, I can't take it. I need sleep or I'm going to go crazy." Steve got out of bed in a huff, while I cried, and then I heard two loud smacking sounds and Maxi let out a blood curdling scream. The scream was horrifying to hear, A hot electric energy shot through my body like a lightning bolt. I was out of bed within an instant. My head swirled with pressure as I stumbled over to Maxi, scooped him up into my arms and ran out of the bedroom. I sat down by the staircase while Maxi clung to me tightly. I'd never heard him scream like that before and it frightened me. I couldn't comprehend what had happened. His body was stiff as a board and his wailing wouldn't subside regardless of my attempts to calm and console him. Something felt very wrong; I just wasn't aware of the magnitude yet.

Eventually his screaming began to subside and slow into gagging sobs; meanwhile, he still clutched me tight. Possibly twenty minutes had past, when I saw in horror what had happened. Maxi's bare back had two large hand prints, each one bearing the impression of five fingers! I felt my body go limp with shock! I didn't want to freak out and frighten Maxi more; however, I cried out, "Steve, what did you do?" Steve came out of the room and saw his son's back; his face was sorrowful. And, on that evening, something within little Maxi switched off.

The following morning, I was unsure of what I should do. The two hand prints had now turned to bruised hand prints. I felt responsible for Maxi's condition and ached inside with uncertainty. I picked up the phone and did something I had never done before. I called a crisis help hotline.

The woman's caring voice instructed me to leave. "We'll find a home for you and your son," she kindly informed me. *Surely Steve didn't mean to. He looked like he felt sincerely sorry.* My mind mulled it over several times. Not able to think for myself— a scared, wounded woman dealing now with an emotionally and physically wounded son. Sadly, I didn't take the woman's solid, and loving advice.

A Second Surprise

One day, I felt a familiar queasiness. I knew the feeling well enough and thought, *No, it can't be.* Yes, my doctor confirmed I was already three months along with my second child. I feared how Steve would take the news again. He wouldn't touch or talk to me for nearly the entire pregnancy when I was pregnant with Maxi. Surprisingly, he took the news well and was looking forward to another child.

It was the summer of ninety-six. I've mentioned before, being one of Jehovah's Witnesses was beyond challenging. No matter how determined I was, I simply couldn't measure up to their unattainable high standards. My religion was like my marriage: controlling and impossible. My nerves continued electrically shorting in and out like water thrown onto an electrical appliance. Sleep deprivation added to my gradual debilitation. And now, I was pregnant with my second child.

They say life is like a giant wheel which continues to propel forward. In my case, I felt as though I were spiraling out of control and into a deep void of black.

Disapproving Eyes

My religion caused an enormous amount of my anxiety. For instance, when at the congregation, our children are to be seen, not heard. If they made too much noise, we were instructed to take them out back and spank them. There was no provision of entertainment for our children, such as some churches call a Sunday School: a separate room for them to sing about God, draw pictures, and learn about the Bible in a fun way. We were taught that Sunday Schools weren't appropriate.

Steve would bring large books filled with glossy photos of cars for Maxi's distraction. I'd get "the look" from elders and would be questioned afterwards about the books. "The only pictures Maxi should be looking at, are from the Bible story book," they'd reprimand.

I feel in confidence, that I speak in behalf of all congregation members, not only are the parents stressed out trying to keep their children calm, most importantly, our children are deeply frustrated beyond what is even close to being natural. Not all parents were heavy handed with their children, but the majority were. I felt sick and repulsed seeing little ones taken out back and beaten because of their natural restless nature. Often, parents took their personal frustrations out on their children. I remember a brother commenting to Steve one Sunday, "I don't like causing a scene by taking my son out back. So, I just casually reach over, and rap him upside his head with my knuckle. He gets the point really quick," he chuckled.

Unfortunately, Steve took the advice and added his own spin to it. One evening at one of our bible studies, Maxi sat on my left side and Steve on my right. I gave him crayons and paper, after nearly two hours. he eventually was bored, and restless Steve reached over me, it appeared as if he tapped Maxi on his thigh. He let out a loud, unexpected scream! He grabbed onto the inside of his thigh while tears streamed down his cheeks. Quickly, I grabbed him into my arms and whispered into Steve's ear, "What did you do?" "I pinched him," I asked him to pinch me as hard as he had pinched Maxi because I needed to know just how hard he pinched. Steve smiled, gave an approving nod, and pinched my arm. I about came unstitched. I stood up and went straight to the bathroom. Maxis face was red as he continued crying, ordinarily we are supposed to clasp are hands over our child's mouth to muffle their cries. And pull your hand off each time their ready to take a breath. For myself it always felt like torture. I pulled Maxis hand off his thigh to investigate and was horrified to see a dime-sized blood blister had already formed!

Immediately I was filled with a sensation that started at my feet, traveled up my legs, my stomach, my chest, and stopped at my throat. It choked me with hot rage. More than anything, I desired to unleash my unheard voice—my shrill screams of protest! If I were to compare myself with a fictional character you would have seen an angry dragon spewing forth fiery rage. It felt as though my explosive, pent-up screams could have easily leveled the room around me. I hated Steve for his cruelty and insensitivity. It was crazy, how I could have such rage coursing through me and yet still tenderly hold little Maxi in my arms, while gently rubbing his thigh and consoling him.

The penetrating glares of obsessed followers were nearly impossible for me to ward off, mainly because I took all glares to heart and tried pleasing everyone around me, having their approval and acceptance was paramount. The stiff-necked stubborn ones from my clan, rejected my form of discipline; their glaring eyes rolled with ease. I couldn't bring myself to use the cruel punishment of the wooden spoon as my Mom had or the belt that my Dad used. My philosophy was if I needed to give Maxi an occasional pop on the butt, I'd only use my hand.

The pressure was constant to be at five Bible studies a week, and in the Saturday preaching. One, evening after dinner, I got myself and Maxi dressed. He naturally became agitated, because he didn't want to go, (can you blame him? Its torture for a young child.) Sometimes, he'd run outside to hide. And I'd get more anxious, "We need to be there early, Maxi. We can't be late."

We're instructed to show up early, to mingle, and go home late, for the same reason. We were also instructed to study the material ahead of time and look up all scriptures. The haughty ones would usually use bright neon markers so those around them knew who studied and who didn't. They'd hold their material high enough for all to see. Sometimes, at a frenzied pace, I'd underline my reading material minutes before we'd leave home, I had absolutely no idea what I was studying.

We're instructed to raise our hands regularly and share personal comments. The congregation members were regularly told to be in service, (which was the door to door preaching.) The guilt put on everyone's shoulders was a heavy burden, especially if we weren't putting in enough hours. I spent an average of twelve hours a month, which is challenging with a four-year old and while pregnant with my second. Some took their preaching work to an extreme! One sister drove her car while breast feeding her newborn baby. Nothing was going to slow her down.

I wanted to make the preaching work fun and adventurous for Maxi. He enjoyed opening and closing every gate and ringing every door bell. He giggled when petting purring cats and laughed when splashing his hands in water fountains. Maxie's favorite time was, the mid-morning donut break. Everyone's for that matter!

I usually tried to pioneer two times a year in addition to my usual hours. What that means is filling out a formal contract, stating your agreement to preach fifty hours, which is then signed and dated. An elder then makes a special announcement to the congregation, saying the name of the person pioneering. Everyone gives those pioneering a round of applause, while they turn in their seats and smile approving nods.

For some reason, my name was never announced five years in a row. It crushed my feelings every time my name was not called out. I never would have thought of questioning the elders. So, silently I hurt and the lump in my throat grew. *You're not preaching for the recognition Aubrianna, you're doing it to please Jehovah*, I constantly reminded myself.

I volunteered to pioneer in the month of September. It was 8:00AM and the morning was already warm. I got out of bed after having had roughly three hours of sleep. My pregnant body ached. I contemplated staying home, but I was pioneering so that wasn't going to happen. I stocked my book bag and made sure my Bible and the latest *Watch Tower* and *Awake* articles were in it. I grabbed an apple, some graham crackers and a sippy cup with juice for Maxi. I dressed in a blue skirt and matching top, then slipped into my nylons and high heels.

Maxie munched on an apple while we drove to the Kingdom Hall and parked on cedar street. Because I was running a few minutes late I was agitated and nervous, I couldn't handle seeing the critical, disapproving facial expressions, from congregation members whenever anyone was late. I felt emotional as though I'd cry at any given moment. Maxi's warm and caring little hand reassured me as we walked into the building. And, as expected certain ones turned in their seats and gave me "The Look." And, once again guilt gripped me, and far, far too often.

Our congregation had a regional preacher and his wife visiting us. They come to encourage and support the Kingdom Hall members, to stay committed and to not give up their dedication. Soon, car groups were formed, and I was told I'd be working with the preacher's wife, *GULP*! She looked like the uptight sort, which only made me more nervous. We stepped outside, while fifteen or twenty of us mingled and chatted before we departed in the preaching work. The preacher's wife looked me up and down, as though she'd bitten into something sour and wasn't sure where to spit it out.

She stepped forward and asked my name. "Aubrianna," I nervously replied.

"Well, Aubrianna, first off I would like to say: I don't think your skirt is appropriate to wear in service. It's too short. I think you need to go home and change into something that doesn't show so much of your legs."

I looked down at my skirt which had managed to hike slightly above my knees, revealing my long lovely legs. I replied, "Oh, I'm sorry. That can be fixed." I self-consciously tugged my skirt down over my knees. Her smug expression didn't change, as she shifted her gaze to Maxi and gave him the once over.

"Hmm," she chirped, "he seems to have a lot of energy."

"Yes, he's my exuberant little man," I cheerfully replied, trying to hide my nervousness.

When I walked to the mini-van and opened the door to put Maxi in his car seat, Maxi's unfinished apple he'd been munching on earlier rolled out of the van and into the street. I felt a flush of embarrassment as heat rushed over my cheeks, quickly I scooped it up, and hoped no one saw what had happened.

Soon the three of us were belted into the minivan and ready to go. I was having difficulty breathing and knew it was going to be a very long morning. We soon arrived at the street we'd be working. We began walking to the first door and Maxi excitedly charged ahead of me. Sometimes, he was too impatient to wait for me and he'd ring the doorbell before I was even there. Usually however, he patiently waited. But this morning he didn't! If I had to guess, I'd say either "Mommy Dearest" had never been a Mother, or she lacked the Mothering instincts big time! She wouldn't let Maxi ring the door bells or open and shut the gates. I politely asked if she'd let Maxi ring the next-door bell. She reacted as though she was having a tooth pulled.

Moments later, my exuberant Maxi found a long stick and began walking to a fence to play "tunes." His face lit up with a bright smile! "Ma Ma can we play tunes?" And, that was about the time "Mommy Dearest" came unglued. She looked at me as though I were raising a monster. She shook her head and spoke an irritated blast! "Okay, okay, okay, this has got to stop now! You can't let your son behave like this! Just look at him. For one thing, his hair is too long. He should have a haircut. He looks more like a girl, and his shirt has already pulled out of his pants. And, now he's playing with a stick? We represent Jehovah when we're preaching. Jehovah would not be pleased! This is not my idea of a good example!"

My eyes enlarged with worry. I quickly kneeled before Maxi and tried yanking down my skirt, so she wouldn't accuse me a second time of showing to much leg. Nervously my hands trembled as I tucked Maxi's white shirt back into his navy-blue trousers and ran my fingers through his blonde locks and behind his ears. I tried reasoning with a loving yet very nervous reply,

"The stick is a game we've been playing since he was just a baby and his hair is so beautiful, it's not long like a girls hair."

Her expression hadn't changed as she blasted a second time. "Either get him under control or we finish now!" So, I desperately tried keeping Maxi under control. Which meant he couldn't ring door bells, put his fingertips in the water fountains, pet cats, pick up a stick, or even so much as open a gate. Needless to say, our morning finished early; "Mommy Dearest" had had ENOUGH!

That evening, Steve, Maxi, and I entered the Kingdom Hall for Bible study. This was also the night special announcements were made for those putting extra hours in the preaching work. Halfway through our Bible discussion, an elder went up on stage to make his announcement before the congregation. After each name was called, the brothers and sisters gave their approval with loud applause. My heart needed the recognition; I ached for love and acceptance. *Maybe this time*, I silently pleaded. *Maybe this time.* Once again, my name was not mentioned. I swallowed hard, the lump in my throat felt like a boulder, while tears pricked at the corners my eyes. I fought back the urge to run out of the room, or cry in front of all these people. *Please don't cry Aubri, please don't cry*, I silently begged.

Elder Rod Realer approached Steve and me after the service. Steve wasn't one to speak up for me, so I was shocked when I heard him say, "So Rod, why wasn't Aubrianna's name announced on stage? She's pioneering this month."

Rod lowered his voice, "Oh, well you see, we elder's feel Aubrianna doesn't keep Maxi clean enough." (For the record, I kept Maxi not only clean, but dressed adorably. It was common for tourists regularly to take pictures of him, stating how beautiful he was. However, the only difference was I wasn't the sort of Mother that would freak out if my son wanted to splash in water fountains or pick up sticks.) Elder Rod continued to speak, "He should probably have a haircut and the minivan isn't clean enough. Why, just this morning, an apple rolled out of her van. We should always represent Jehovah in a clean way. She can still donate her fifty-five hours, we just won't make the announcement."

Silently, I stood listening to his strangling uncaring words and accusations. They stabbed me severely, like that, of a frozen dull knife! I stood in silence, I no longer heard any words from Elder Rod or anyone around me. A strange numbing pain grabbed my chest (heart region) it felt as though I became unplugged. A strange unraveling with in me began a descent (or was it ascent?) a feeling that was foreign, a feeling beyond words.

Melt Down

And so, on that hot summer evening, something deep within my core gradually unraveled. Steve dropped me off at the house just a few minutes before 10:00PM. While he and Maxi went to his parents. "We'll be back in an hour," he stated.

Silently, and in a state of frozen confusion, I stood in the darkened hallway void of any light, except for that of soft moon beams trickling through the window.

Standing in stillness, I stared blankly, at the walls encircling me, my cage. Feeling as I had my entire life: unloved, alone, abused, misunderstood, and now? Shattering into millions of frozen pieces! From deep within my core, heat rushed to the surface like a volcano ready to erupt. Fires from accumulated emotional traumas and years of abuse; pushed, burned, and forced their way up and out like lava! The caged bird screeched out a final distressing plea.

"Doesn't anyone understand me? I just want to be loved! Please, wont someone love me? "Oh, my God! Oh, my God! **Oh...My...Goddddd!!!"**

My body shook with frenzy! My legs trembled beneath me. While sobbing out my unheard frustrations, I grabbed onto the staircase railing and climbed the stairs to the bathroom. The moon shone through the window casting a soft glow as I stood before the mirror and stared into the eyes of a stranger... Or, was it me? I didn't know anymore... Did I ever know?

About the Author

Aubrianna lives, in beautiful Northern California. Her greatest ambition is inspiring and motivating those of us ready for transformation. Her sincerest desires are helping children, adolescents, liberating men, women, and through God's grace, bringing back equilibrium to our magnificent earth.

She is a Native American healer, an ordained Minister, a Reiki Master, she has a passion for dream interpretations, numerology, dancing, singing and living life joyfully.

Aubrianna Rose Will not Leave You Hanging!

In her sequels, *Learning to Fly book two, and Flying In Love book three.* Discover how long it takes for Aubri to finally say, "ENOUGH!" Compelling events will dramatically unfold, one shocking layer at a time.

Of course, there will still be adventures in every corner. Such as, what happened the day Aubri felt an odd sensation tickling down her spine and urging her to investigate the cabinet calling to her.

Nancy Drew dragged a seven-foot metal ladder across the garage floor as it scraped an oddly familiar sound. Cautiously she climbed to the top, opened the cabinet door, peered inside, and gasped out loud, **"Oh My God"**!

Learn how she eventually connects with her inner guidance, how she heals from past traumas, how she gains health. And, learn how she grabs onto the Divine "hand" of assistance waiting for her, to simply ask for help. Learn how she receives help from Divine and Synchronistic teachers, as the expression says: "when the student is ready the teachers will come."

v

Made in the USA
San Bernardino, CA
25 June 2019